MR TODIWALA'S
BOMBAY

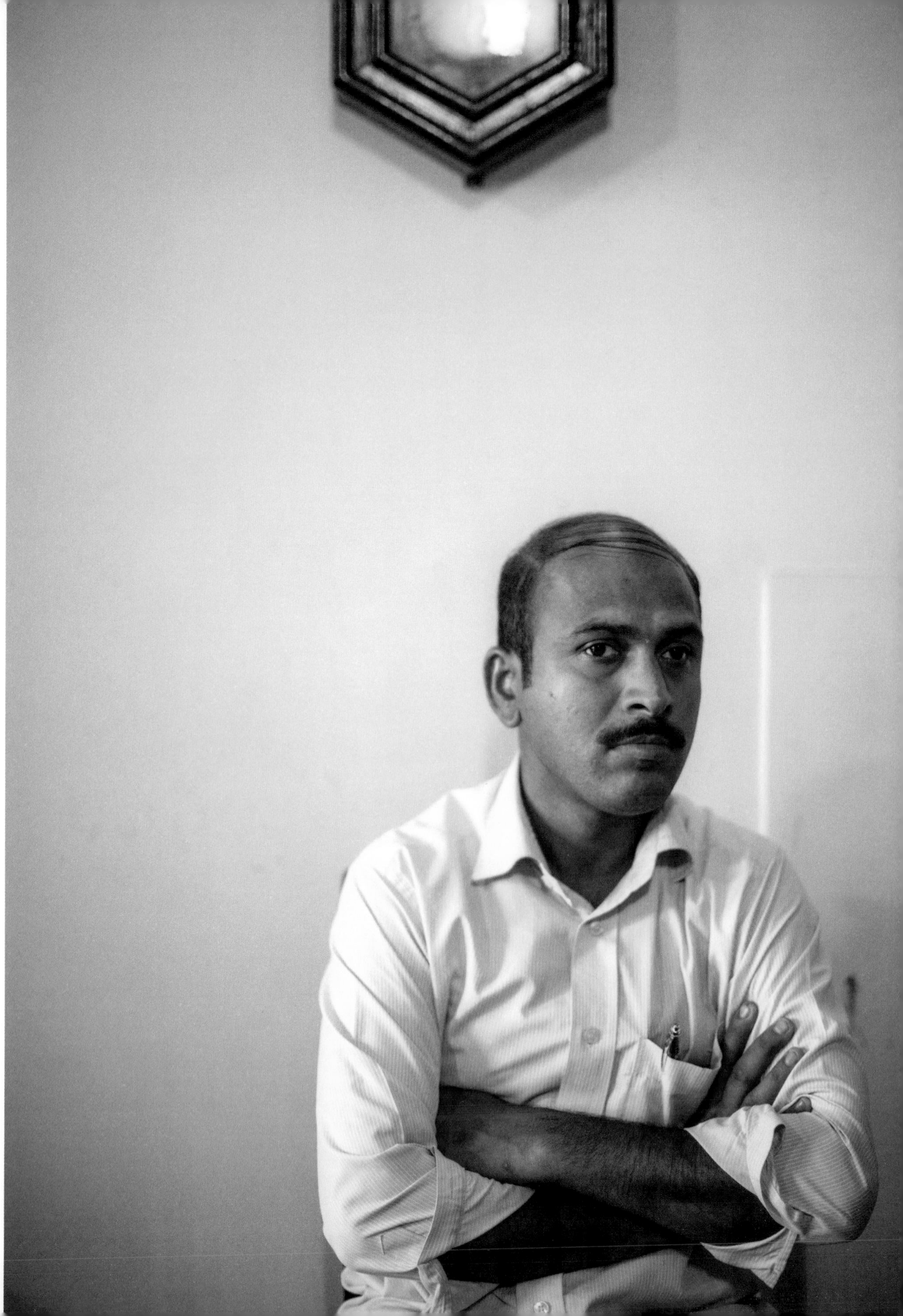

MR TODIWALA'S
BOMBAY

RECIPES & MEMORIES FROM INDIA

CYRUS TODIWALA

PHOTOGRAPHY BY HELEN CATHCART

hardie grant books

MELBOURNE · LONDON

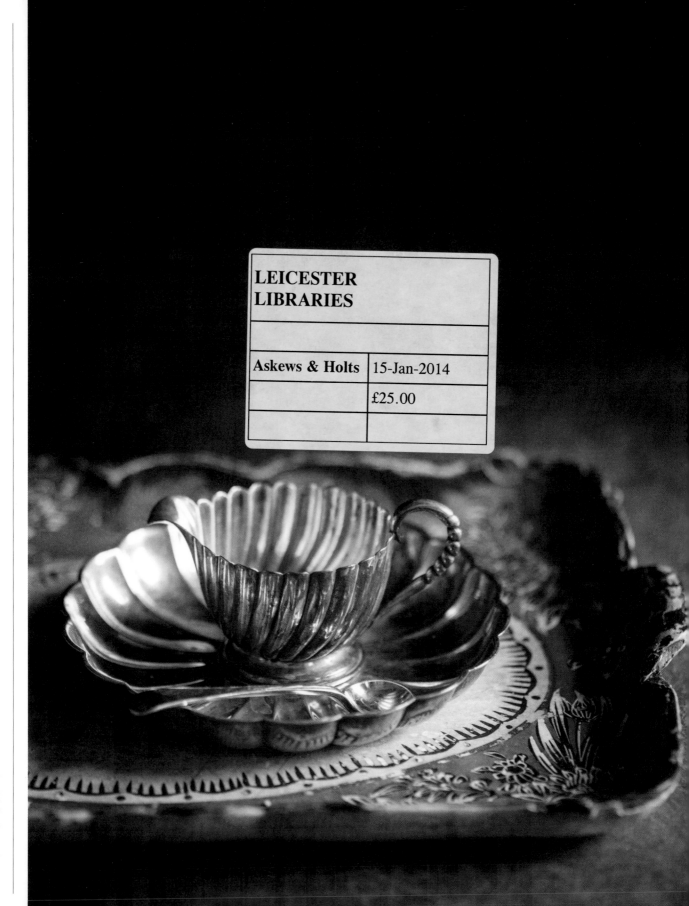

MR TODIWALA'S BOMBAY

CONTENTS

'Oh Bombay, my Bombay' is a phrase that has graced many a song. Another is, 'A little careful, a little watchful, this is Bombay my dear'. The city was originally made up of seven islands joined by causeways, but was transformed into the metropolis it is today in the 18th century. The Portuguese invaded and named it Bombaiyya (A Good Bay), which the British shortened to Bombay. It is now called Mumbai after Mumbadevi, the goddess of the fisherfolk who used to inhabit the islands, but to many of us it is still Bombay and always will be (though, of course, we refer to it as Mumbai when we are talking colloquially!).

Throughout its history, it has been populated by migrants from other parts of the subcontinent, from small fiefdoms ruling certain, islands and neighbouring lands to those seeking wealth due to its fabulous location. Even today it is believed that thousands pour into Bombay daily trying to find that pot of gold they think is awaiting their arrival. Most stay and eke out a basic survival rather than go back to their villages, either because life in Mumbai is actually better than where they came from or because they simply cannot afford to return home. The crawling metropolis has an unofficial claimed population of over 22 million. It is not only India's great capital of finance and business but also to me and millions of us Bombaywallas the best city in the country and, for most, the world.

Bombay is the city where I was born and one that holds many powerful memories for me. Although I suffered from acute asthma, my childhood was filled with fun and happiness. Growing up with an extended family with a popular, well-known father and an equally popular maternal uncle, I had the honour and privilege of meeting hundreds of people and learning a lot as I grew up. My uncle used our sitting and dining room for his afternoon dispensary where tons of patients came to be treated by the one they considered an angel sent by God to heal and cure. Such was his following that people would sit on the steps of the building all night whilst my uncle slept because they wanted only to be treated by him!

My dad was the first Indian to work for the Western India Automobile Association and was its first Indian Chief of Road Service, working closely with Bombay's police and other authorities. He was a respected, well-liked and well-connected member of the community. In 1968 we moved out of our apartment when the building (or Cabinet House as it was called) was sold and later demolished to make way for a new block, and into a house in Bandra, a suburb of Bombay. It was where my father had previously lived in 1938 with his two aunts whom he looked after until they passed away. It has been our home in Bombay ever since. I also spent three years in my uncle's home in Madhya Pradesh – a state in central India – where the dry climate suited my asthma and where, once again, the local fare influenced me greatly. It was the extended family that first gave me my taste for good food. Meals cooked by mum at home, the cooking of our neighbours and local street food have all influenced my cooking – and still do to this day. Each time we go back to Bombay, I learn something new.

My great aunt made awesome chapattis, mince-filled potato cakes and many other things. Her spiced lamb mince was famous in the family along with her chutneys and pickles. I will always remember her raw cane syrup, too. It was like dark treacle and was the one thing that, as kids, we were all addicted to. My mum was also an expert at making chapattis and it was amazing how round she got them and how they rotated while she rolled them out. I have never been able to emulate her skill. A particular fond memory is how, at a very young age, we enjoyed caramelized stale chapattis (leftover ones, sautéed in a pan with butter and sugar until golden) and, when I was older, I used to make them for – and then sell them to – my cousins and sister!

Bombay is nothing short of a melting pot of cultures and cuisines. Street food is vast and boasts more intricate fusions than other Indian cities known for their cuisine such as Delhi, Calcutta, Chennai, Lucknow, Bangalore and Hyderabad. Whilst each and every one of them is unique and offers amazing street fare, Mumbai – or our Bombay – surpasses all by its sheer quantity, variety and creativity.

The area surrounding our first house when we lived with our extended famiy, was lined with street food vendors. In those days, it was not, of course, as busy and mad as it is today and the number of outlets has multiplied tenfold. What is great to see, however, is that some of the old establishments are still there fifty years on.

One thing that does amaze me is the amount of spare cash youngsters seem to have to spend these days. When I think back to my childhood and teenage years, money was so scarce that we would walk a few bus stops to save enough to buy a hot *Batata Wada* (see page 166) and a cup of chai (see page 256). Those of us who grew up there in the sixties and seventies, embracing the city and its cultures and vibes, now find it, at times, too expensive for words. However the charm, excitement, flavours and choices have never dwindled but, in fact, quadrupled.

My love of food did, eventually, lead me to join a catering college – the Basant Kumar Somani Polytechnic – and to qualifications, which then led to an amazing, fun-filled, often scary and disappointing, exciting and rewarding career. Whilst catching up with some of my old student friends recently, I was reminded of some of my tomfoolery and mischief. They recalled how we duped our Indian bulk-cookery teacher. My friend Arun Alvares and I always volunteered for everything and she always said how nice we were but we always had an underlying motive, too. Every time we went to collect the chickens for the class from the stores, the livers, gizzards, necks and hearts miraculously vanished and she was left in a quandary. Of course they had been frittered away to prepare a meal for our fellow accomplices and we would have a feast later. One day I overheard her shouting at the storekeeper to complain to the supplier that he was cheating and his chicken should always come with the giblets inside. He, quite rightly, hotly denied it. She cottoned on eventually, but the forced wall-washing and scouring of pots and pans did nothing to suppress the satisfaction of all those yummy treats we had had.

Soon Arun's and my reputation for mischief went before us and if anything went wrong the Principal always called us into her office. Proving our innocence became the greatest battle! Many such memories flood my head as soon as we sit and reminisce in the right company surrounded by friends, food and drink and the great times we used to have. However the love for cooking did not start in college. I used to dabble with my mother in her kitchen all the time (where everything got eaten without complaint), from about twelve years of age. However it was at boarding school that I got my first opportunity to cook.

Our food at school was dismal to say the least and, naturally, for boarders who had adequate exercise, growing bones and ever-empty bellies, something had to be done to feed those hunger pangs. The only time this could be done was in the wee hours of the morning, say between 3 and 4 o'clock. To hatch plans was easy and to invite contributions was easy, too, since we shared it all. Now just bear in mind that our weekly pocket money was just 2 rupees, which, in today's sterling conversion is 0.02p and in India not worth mentioning as even beggars would throw it back at you if you gave them such a paltry amount! A stove had to be smuggled in and, of course, kerosene to light it. We had plenty of allies in school amongst the dinner staff who would do things for a little tip and they became our partners in this mischief – or crime if you wish to call it that. We gave them 10 rupees for a stove and 1 rupee for a litre of kerosene. Smoke had to be avoided as our housemaster was a genius at catching us out and I have had many a stove confiscated. I'm not sure why he never started a catering business: he must have taken at least six off me and many more from the other dormitories!

Remember we were desperate to feed ourselves: leftover bread, sometimes spread with horrible margarine, and half-eaten crusts were stuffed into pockets and delivered to me in the dorm. Milk was always a can of Milkmaid sweetened condensed milk (1.5 rupees) and anything we thought would make a good porridge or bread gruel. Everything went into an old oil tin, which was kept well-hidden in the toilets, with the bread, milk, some water, some coffee powder, raw fruits – mostly guavas from nearby trees or purple fruit called *jaambul* in India and the porridge session would begin. I would be in charge of these culinary exploits and a few would be watching out for the ever-nosey Mr Gadre who always seemed to have an instinct that something was up.

The porridge would be divided to all who woke up at that unearthly hour, devoured, everything washed up and stowed away, the stove hidden well in someone's trunk, phenol splashed around to eradicate the smell of kerosene and cooking and we went back to sleep until the wake-up bell at 6 am. I am not sure if I would eat our creations today as I am not, exactly, desperate for food now but what days they were … super!

A distant relative also had a hotel in this little hill station convalescent town of Devlali (or Deolali as the British spelt it when it was an army camp – and, incidentally, where the term 'doolally' came from, originally referring to men who had so-called 'doolally tap' or 'camp fever', an apparent madness whilst waiting for ships back to Britain after a stint of duty in India). Each month I was allowed to spend one weekend with them. The Coronation Hotel had a typical British-style dining atmosphere and each guest came to the dining room for breakfast, lunch and dinner (all bookings were full board then). Here I spent several hours of those weekends watching the cooks work and learnt a lot.

MR BAKER

Training in Bombay gave me some amazing insights into how different establishments operate as we moved from hotels to restaurants to outdoor catering options and so on. Money was never on the agenda: we often got grossly exploited but it was fun.

During this time my love of baking had grown and very soon I became known in college as 'Mr Baker'. One day we (Arun and I) were asked to make some fruit cakes for an East Indian wedding. This turned into a small business, working into the very wee hours of the morning making the cakes, then cutting, slicing, packing and delivering them all before going off to college in the mornings.

After I started working full-time as a young chef at the Taj Mahal Hotel, I still continued with the baking and had several orders on the go at any one time. Mum and Dad were conscripted as unpaid workers because I had a long day at work, leaving at 7 or 8 in the morning and not returning before midnight so I had to rely on their help. They would line my tins, weigh out my ingredients and keep everything ready before they retired to bed. I would come home, freshen up and work until maybe 2 or 3 am and then retire. The cakes were baked in several box ovens. Only older folk will know what I am talking about here but these were little tin boxes with a door and shelves that sat on top of your cooker and the gas rings below heated the ovens. When you were done you simply put the cakes to cool, picked the boxes up and stacked them. The process was very slow but effective although the boxes were always lopsided so we had to chock them up on one side so the cakes remained level.

When my parents rose in the morning, they would pick the cakes up from cooling racks all over the house and put them on the table where I would slice them up after breakfast and Mum would pack them. Dad left for work early and most often we left together then the caterer would come and collect the cakes later from my mum. This was really tiring but when you are young the world is at your feet, and I did feel invincible in those days, little appreciating, of course, the timeless support my parents gave me. Without them and their unflinching efforts, I would have achieved zero!

I did end up making a bit of money so I bought a large cooking range with an oven to accommodate more cakes in one go. Mum loved her new oven, too, as that helped her to make her Granu Toast (as they are lovingly called thanks to my nephew and niece naming them) to perfection. Did I tell you about our toasts? These are a Todiwala Family symbol and Mum is the immortal creator of these. Even today, friends and neighbours ask me when we go to Bombay if I can make them. My sister still does them and here's how they are made: you need to wake up 4.30 am (my parents always rose early but my mum had to because she had to make at least fifty of these toasts, which we gobbled down with abandon for breakfast). Very thinly sliced good quality, old-fashioned, dense, stale bread, as you would for Melba toast, and first lightly toast it very slowly on a griddle-type toaster or a flap-door toaster (if you are lucky enough to still have one as they are now extinct I think!). Spread well with butter and let the semi-toasts rest for a while. Then place on a baking tray, well spread out, and bake in the oven at 120°C/240°F/gas ½ until golden brown and butter is bubbling on the surface. This is a killer for those in fear of raised cholesterol but awesome with scrambled eggs ... I mean real scrambled eggs not ones near omelette consistency!

DIVERSIFICATION

I digress – I was too busy drooling over the thought of Mum's sensational toasts ...

The cake business led to me being asked if I could also get the caterer cheaper wine for the toasting of the wedding ceremony etc. Now, in those days, wine was not readily available and the fortified ones gave you a kick like that from an agitated donkey. So I bought an English book on home wine-making and got into wine production. Well I had two unpaid employees, albeit part time, so I could not complain. We had a spare room in the house so between Dad and me we built a long stand on which five 100-litre drums were placed and we were off. Mum and Dad lost a few friends in the bargain due to the awful smell in the house and the newly-attracted bees and flies for which we had to build new protective systems. That room had the first mesh curtain erected in an Indian home.

I made sweetened wine as Indians primarily do not enjoy dry wines and, besides, it hid the flaws. The resultant strained must (the fermenting fruit pulp left when the juice has been extracted for the wine) was used as fertilizer for our garden but the crows loved it so we ended up having to dig it in always in the dead of night to avoid attack by these crazed, drunken creatures.

At this time I was also going for early morning auctions to the wholesale market to buy my sultanas, candied peel and other dried fruits for the cakes. One morning I noticed that Indian vendors and wholesalers were drinking fresh orange and sweet lime juice. The juice stalls always had piles of citrus peel lying about and I saw this as an opportunity to make my own candied peel. Well you guessed it right – the candied peel business was on soon after! Mum, the poor thing, was on duty watching the slow bubbling syrup. I hired local kids for a little bit of pocket money to come and, with a teaspoon, scrape off all the white pith. Sugar I bought wholesale, anyway, but I also landed up with more peel than I needed. So what now? I sold it to my college and to other vendors and gave them great deals for uncut peel.

This then led to yet another business since now the wholesale fruiterers knew me and whenever they could not sell over ripe pineapples, guavas and so on they asked me if I could use them. I would say no but offer to buy them if they gave me a very good deal and then I said I would give them to my neighbours. But would I give good fruit away? Of course not! Let's make jam, I thought. Once again my long-suffering parents got roped in and, believe you me, they never complained. Their house was hijacked, it looked like a factory and smelt like one, but their support for me was unflinching. All this time I was working full time at the Taj Mahal Hotel learning more skills and getting new ideas all the time.

Eventually all this had to stop as the work pressure and the tiredness got the better of me. Actually, the decision was made for me when I was badly bitten by a crazed Doberman and the temporary disability brought about a collapse.

BACK TO THE DAY JOB

Working at the Taj Mahal Hotel was pretty prestigious for a young, budding chef but, boy, was the pay scale poor and therefore I needed the income from my other exploits to fund the life of a city boy. The Taj, one has to say, gave me the platform to learn and hone my skills. Hard work, yes, and, in today's world, it would be considered serious exploitation with no sympathy for our situation, but I loved it and I soon worked my way to the top, gaining valuable knowledge and managerial abilities right up until the day I left.

But then the Taj gave me something truly special. This pretty young girl called Pervin came in for industrial training with her college and was enamoured by my kitchen. How the rest happened I know not, but we have been married now for 28 years and have two sons, Jamsheed and Hormuzd. We are still together despite the madness of our ventures and my idiosyncrasies, and Pervin has been an invaluable support to me throughout. Our sons are also now involved in the business and, while we put no pressure on them, their interest in it is growing.

Besides my family and friends, cousins and relatives, the Taj Mahal Hotel left an everlasting indelible mark on us and to this day we still always call it 'our Taj'. That said, baking was my first cooking love and my passion has never waned, thanks to my parents' support. There are many more stories I could tell, some hilarious, but that's for another time or in my memoirs if I write them some day.

MY BELOVED BOMBAY

All I can say is that Bombay was where I developed, if nothing else, my crazy habit of over-working but I was always excited and enthusiastic like a small child (which I still am at heart). The city has what it takes to be immortal, contagious, mad, heart-warming, exciting, and bountiful in food and culture. It is a place with which one has a love-hate relationship. It remains intriguing and mysterious, busy yet relaxing, expensive and yet cheap enough on the streets to feed the poor and less fortunate. But, above all, in spite of its magnitude and populace, it is one of the world's safest cities to be out and about in. Please don't take my word for it, ask its residents.

Bombay is steeped in history it also offers entertainment and cuisines second to none. In this book I share with you favourite recipes from my life in this remarkable city, to give you just a taste of what my beloved Bombay has to offer.

SNACKS

The mere word snack has so many different meanings globally. For instance in the UK we might imagine it to be a platter of sandwiches, some biscuits, quiches, sausage rolls or some other fried tit-bits. In the Far East, most cultures snack all day but what they are eating is actually small portions of proper food.

In the sub continent of India the snack culture gives you the feeling that this is the common religion of its masses. The streets are continuously buzzing with food vendors, from the wee hours of the morning to late into the night always hawking, always beckoning, always creating and offering what I deem to be the vastest (if there be such a word) array of little bits produced anywhere in the world.

One can lose track of course and find that they have over eaten between meals and the main meal is yet to come. One can also lose oneself in that gay abandon of lust for eating delicious-looking, tempting and not-so-healthy scrumptious delights. Feasting is the evil, fasting is the forgotten promise and health is banished with a wave when you get that all-powerful invincible feeling that you are indestructible.

The variety of snacks in India is so vast that it would take me five lifetimes to perhaps cover 50 per cent of them, but what we have covered in the book are some of our favourites from Bombay our bad, berserk, out-of-control, totally gourmandizing, absolutely fabulous city.

Snacking forms a daily part of the Mumbaikars or Bombaywalla's life. The snacks range from very cheap to extremely expensive to those that we attack, the good value types! In the home, snacking is not un-common and it is the women that are the great creators of some of the tastiest treats known to mankind. The pride of India's talent is often in the domestic world behind closed doors where mothers, wives, aunts, grandmas and sisters are all working away making an array of snacks for their loved ones, snacks which chefs like myself would yearn to learn and introduce to others. Women pride themselves in their own secret formulas and every son and husband, brother and admirer will claim that his maker is the best of the best.

For me the Gujarati woman is the one to envy! She is probably the best-trained daughter or daughter-in-law in whose home food is once again the overarching religion. These great women make virtually everything themselves and will put the greatest chefs amongst us to severe shame.

I wish I could bring you many more snack recipes but perhaps next time round. Meanwhile make, cook and delight yourselves in the magnificent world of Indian snacks.

For the masala

2 thin green chillies

6–8 sprigs of coriander (cilantro)

2 garlic cloves

1 cm (½in) piece of fresh ginger

½ tsp cumin seeds

¼ tsp salt

pinch of ground turmeric

For the omelette

4 eggs, separated

1 tsp plain (all purpose) flour

2 tsp sunfloweror rapeseed oil

knob of butter (optional)

To serve

sweet chutney and

buttered warm *pain rustique*

BHUJELO PORO

BAKED SPICY OMELETTE

Serves 2–4

This omelette is a Parsee speciality originating from Gujarat and should be eaten as soon as it is baked. Whatever you wish to eat with it, be it toast, hot soft bread or croissants, should all be kept ready. For breakfast a really fruity jelly is ideal.

The Parsee would have their omelette with an extra dollop of butter as well (and this I would recommend, though not on health grounds!).

Grind the masala ingredients to a smooth paste in a mortar with a pestle (or a small bowl with the end of a rolling pin). Alternatively use a clean coffee grinder or small food processor, adding a splash of water, if necessary. Take care you don't add too much, though, and make it runny.

Preheat the oven to 220°C/425°F/gas 7.

Beat the egg whites until very stiff and fluffy. Mix the egg yolks together with the flour and masala paste, loosening with a splash more water, if necessary, then gently fold into the egg whites.

Heat the oil in a large, 25 cm (10 in) non-stick ovenproof frying pan or flame-proof baking dish. When the oil is hazy but not smoking, add in the egg mixture and spread out.

Dot the butter over the top, if using, and, after a minute or two, when just browning on the base, place the pan into the oven.

Bake for 5–10 minutes or until the omelette is risen and golden brown on the top, cooked through, light and fluffy. To check whether it is cooked, insert a clean knife into the centre of the omelette and see if it comes out clean.

Cut in halves or quarters and enjoy with sweet chutney, and warm *pain rustique*, soft rolls or toast.

18 chicken wings, wing tip and first joint
removed, leaving meaty end only

5 cm (2 in) piece of fresh ginger,
finely chopped

4 garlic cloves, chopped

3 long, thin green chilies

2–3 tbsp light soy sauce

½ tsp salt, or to taste

vegetable oil for deep-frying

3 eggs, beaten

100–150 g (3½ –5 oz/1–1½ cups)
cornflour (cornstarch)

minced green chilli and red chilli
dipping sauce, to serve

DRUMS OF HEAVEN

DEEP-FRIED CHICKEN WINGS

Makes 18 wings

In India we have a large indigenous Chinese population, mostly immigrants from Hakka who came a few hundred years ago and made India their home. Their cuisine evolved and, much like us Parsees, also took on some key Indian notes. Some Chinese dishes are very street-orientated and often, late at night, handcarts with a wok cooker and a small menu will appear in prime spots catering to a hungry mobile crowd of fans. These crisp-fried Indo-Chinese chicken wings, also known as Chicken Lollipops, served piping hot with minced green chilli and a fiery dip are a favourite for those who long for the chilli fix.

Scrape and push the meat down the wing bone from the meatless end and gather at the bottom but do not dislodge the bone itself. Then, by holding the bone end in one hand, gather all the meat together at the top of the bone by cupping the other hand over the top and pressing the skin inwards to expose the meat on the outside.

After all the wings are prepared, blend the ginger, garlic and green chillies with the soy sauce and salt (remember that soy is salty too) in a bowl large enough to hold the wings. Add the wings and rub them thoroughly in the marinade until everything is well massaged in. Clean the edges of the bowl with a little paper towel, cover and place in the refrigerator to marinate for 3–4 hours.

When ready to fry, heat the oil for deep-frying over a low heat.

Add the eggs to the wings and mix them in, then add the cornflour a little at a time and blend in well until you get a sticky but thick coating all round. The batter has to be dryish and not runny, with the wings clinging to it or, even, stuck together.

Now increase the heat until the oil is 180°C (350°F) or when a tiny bit of the batter when dropped in rises to the surface straight away, sizzling. Keep a colander over a bowl ready for draining the fried wings. Separate the wings if stuck together and fry, a few at a time, until crisp and well-browned. Remove with a slotted spoon, drain well in the colander, then blot on paper towel, if necessary.

Keep hot whilst cooking the remainder and serve hot with minced green chilli and red chilli dipping sauce.

800 g (1 lb 12 oz) boneless chicken
salt and white pepper to taste

For the masala
40 g (1½ oz) fresh ginger,
roughly chopped
40 g (1½ oz) garlic cloves
½ tsp cumin seeds
½ tsp coriander seeds
½ tsp chilli powder
¼ tsp ground turmeric
2 tbsp lime or lemon juice
½ tbsp garam masala
150 ml (5 fl oz/⅔ cup) plain yoghurt
50 ml (2 fl oz/¼ cup) groundnut
or sunflower oil
generous knob of butter, melted

For the mint yoghurt dressing
half a bunch of fresh mint leaves
4–5 heaped tbsp Greek yoghurt
1 tsp sugar
1 green chilli
salt to taste

To serve
kachumber (see page 93),
chapattis (see pages 183 or 185)

MURGH TIKKA

CHICKEN TIKKA

Serves 6 as a snack

The most widely known Indian recipe, this tikka of chicken is a succulent and juicy kebab, and makes an ideal snack or a starter. Tikka simply means 'cube'. It is traditionally cooked in a tandoor but is fine barbecued, grilled (broiled) or, even, baked in the oven. In India we use boneless leg meat but you could use thigh or breast or a mixture of both.

Cut the chicken into bite-sized cubes. Rub in some salt and pepper and set aside.

In a blender or small food processor add all the other ingredients, except the butter, with half the yoghurt and blend to a smooth paste, stopping and scraping down the sides as necessary. Transfer to a bowl and whisk in the remaining yoghurt. Check here for spiciness to suit your palate. Add more chilli if you like the heat.

Add the chicken to the marinade. Mix to coat evenly. Cover and leave to marinate for at least 4–5 hours or overnight in the refrigerator.

Preheat the grill (broiler) or barbecue but make sure it is not too hot or the chicken will burn before it cooks through. Alternatively preheat the oven to 230°C/450°F/gas 8. Thread the meat onto 8 soaked wooden skewers. Lay the skewers on the grill-rack or a rack in a roasting tin and grill (broil) for about 15 minutes or bake for 8–10 minutes until well browned and cooked through, but still juicy and tender, basting with the melted butter and turning occasionally.

To make the mint yoghurt dressing, simply purée all the ingredients together until it becomes smooth in consistency. Season to taste and keep refrigerated until ready to serve.

When the chicken is cooked, serve hot, with the mint dressing, kachumber and chapattis.

30–35 g (1–1¼ oz/ generous ¼ cup)
    chickpea (garbanzo) or besan flour

2 eggs

1 onion, chopped

1 plum tomato, chopped

1 large green chilli, seeded,
    if liked, and chopped

1 tbsp chopped coriander
    (cilantro) leaves

½ tsp ground cumin

¼ tsp ground turmeric

½ tsp chilli powder

1 tsp lemon juice

salt to taste

2–3 tbsp sunflower or rapeseed oil

To serve

hot and sweet chutney, such as mango
    and bread or chapattis (see pages
    183 or 185)

granulated (raw) sugar, for sprinkling
    (optional)

lime juice, for drizzling (optional)

BESAN NO PORO

CHICKPEA FLOUR OMELETTE

Makes 2–3 omelettes

This is a simple masala omelette made with chickpea (garbanzo) flour (also known as besan flour), and eggs. These omelettes can also be eaten along with several of the vegetable dishes on pages 116–145 instead of bread or chapattis. Alternatively, sandwich together with thin slices of cucumber and tomato inside and cut into wedges. For those who don't eat egg, you can follow this recipe using just the chickpea flour.

Sift the chickpea flour in a deep bowl and add enough water to make a smooth paste. Break the eggs in and beat the mixture. Add all the other ingredients and mix well.

Taste and season as desired. The batter should be that of a pancake so it should be the consistency of pouring cream. If too thick you will get a heavy omelette, as it will not spread well in the pan, so add a splash more water, if necessary.

Heat a heavy-based, non-stick frying pan. Add a little oil and tilt to coat the pan. Stir the batter well, add a third or half the batter, depending on the size of your pan. Swirl the pan to coat the base with the batter.

Let one side cook until golden brown underneath over a medium heat. When just set, flip over and cook the other side.

Repeat with the remaining oil and batter to make two or three omelettes. Serve hot with mango chutney, or sprinkle with some sugar and drizzle with lime juice. Alternatively, try spreading the omelette with a little chopped chutney, roll up and eat!

For the tomato sauce

2–3 tbsp sunflower or rapeseed oil

2 x 2.5 cm (1 in) pieces of cinnamon stick

2 large whole dried red chillies, broken into
     three or four pieces (seeded, if liked)

3–4 cloves (optional)

2 smallish onions, finely chopped

1 heaped tbsp ginger and garlic paste (see page 157)
     (or 4 garlic cloves, crushed and 2 tsp
     grated fresh ginger)

4–5 tomatoes, chopped (or a 400 g can
     chopped tomatoes)

1 tbsp malt vinegar

1 tbsp jaggery or muscovado sugar

½ tsp tamarind paste (optional)

salt to taste

For the fish cakes

250 g (9 oz) white fish fillet, skinned

1 large green chilli, finely chopped

2.5 cm (1 in) piece fresh ginger,
     finely chopped

6–8 garlic cloves, finely chopped

2 tbsp chopped coriander (cilantro) leaves

1 tsp salt or to taste

1 tbsp lemon juice

1 egg

2 slices white bread, soaked briefly
     in water and squeezed out

To finish

100 g (3½ oz/scant 1 cup) plain flour

2–3 eggs

oil for shallow-frying

MACHCHI NA CUTLESS

FISH CAKES WITH TOMATO SAUCE

Serves 4

This is a simple fish cake recipe and one which many Parsee mums create out of leftovers so it doesn't have to be copied exactly – adapt it to suit what you have to hand. However, to get a good authentic result, it's worth following it at first so you get to know the cultural differences and can understand the background to the flavourings we use and the likes and dislikes of our Parsee community. The tomato sauce will keep for quite a long time in the refrigerator provided it is kept well covered, you do not insert a wet spoon into it and you keep the edges clean. It is useful to serve with many other foods such as meat or vegetable patties, battered fish, chicken or rice dishes.

First make the tomato sauce. Heat the oil in a heavy-based saucepan or a flame-proof casserole dish, over a medium heat. Add the cinnamon sticks and sauté until deep brown in colour and swollen but not burnt. Add the red chillies and cloves and after about 20 seconds add the chopped onions and sauté gently for 3–4 minutes until they are soft but not brown. Add the ginger and garlic paste and sauté for a further minute or so.

Stir in the tomatoes, vinegar, jaggery and tamarind, if using, part-cover and simmer over a low heat for 15–20 minutes, stirring occasionally, until pulpy. Season to taste with salt, remove from the heat and set aside.

Now prepare the fish cakes. If you have a mincer (grinder) or food processor at home then mincing the fish is easy. If not then you can chop up the fillets and with a cleaver or a large knife chop repeatedly as if chopping parsley until you get a fine mince.

Blend all the chopped ingredients into the mince and mix well almost kneading it to a rough paste.

Add the salt, lemon juice and the egg and mix well. Finally work in the well-squeezed bread. The bread is to stabilise the mix and if you find it is too soft, soak and squeeze another slice or two until you have a mix that is firm enough to form into balls without sticking to your palms.

To check the seasoning, fry a tiny piece fry of the mixture and taste. When you are happy with it, divide the mix into even sized balls depending on the size you prefer. You may like them large if eating as a main dish or small if serving as a snack.

Heat about 5 mm (¼ in) oil in a deep frying pan. Spread the flour out in a flat tray big enough to take all the balls at one time and beat the eggs in a shallow dish.

Flatten each ball until about 1 cm (½ in) thick, smooth the edges so that they or nor jagged or uneven, coat in the flour, then the beaten egg, draining off excess. If the egg is well-beaten you will get a nice frilly texture.

Fry the cakes in batches for 2–3 minutes on each side until golden brown. Drain on paper towels. Remove the cinnamon and cloves from the sauce, if preferred and reheat, if serving hot. Serve the fishcakes hot or cold with the sauce. They are also good served cold in soft rolls as a snack meal like a sandwich.

250 g (9 oz) poha (flattened rice)

2–3 tbsp sunflower or rapeseed oil

½ tsp mustard seeds

¼ tsp cumin seeds

a generous pinch asafoetida (hing)

2–3 garlic cloves, finely chopped

2.5 cm (1 in) fresh ginger piece, peeled
and finely chopped

2 white onions, finely chopped

3–5 green chillies, finely chopped

10–12 curry leaves, shredded

½ tsp ground turmeric

salt to taste

200 g (7 oz) potatoes, peeled and diced
(or 1 large potato)

150–200 g (5–7 oz) green peas
(optional)

juice of 1 small lime (or half if large)

1 tsp caster (superfine) sugar

½ whole coconut, grated or 250 g
(9 oz) frozen grated or

2–3 tbsp desiccated (shredded)
coconut, soaked in water than drained

chilli powder to taste

2 heaped tbsp, chopped fresh coriander
(cilantro) leaves

BATATA POHA

FLATTENED RICE WITH POTATOES

Serves 4

Flattened rice, or poha, is very popular across the subcontinent and it is prepared and cooked in many different ways. Each community has its own style, whether they turn it into sweets, desserts, savoury dishes, snacks or midday quick meals.

This recipe is perfect for a welcoming, light midday snack, if someone turns up at the doorstep unannounced or as a teatime accompaniment. The Maharashtrians call it *Batata Poha*, the Gujerati call it *bataka aney poha bhaat*, and in South India in Tamil Nadu it's often called *aval uppuma*. The Gujerati version may have a bit more sugar and lime juice in it, and perhaps peanuts; the South Indians no doubt have their mustard seeds but also urad or white lentil and/or channa daal (or yellow split peas); however one thing is for certain, this snack is one of my favourites and I can assure you that it is most enjoyable.

Tips: The Maharashtrians also add fried or roasted unsalted peanuts to their Poha. To make it in the South Indian style (*aval uppuma*) add one teaspoon each of urad daal and channa daal after the mustard seeds have cracked and then continue with the rest of the method. Leave out the sugar, lime juice and peanuts. However, fried broken cashew nuts are more than welcome.

Wash the poha or flattened rice well, squeeze out the excess water and drain in a colander.

Heat the oil in a *kadhai*, a shallow but largish lidded frying pan, or casserole dish with a lid.

When the oil forms a haze add the mustard, reduce the heat to medium and place the lid on top for just a few seconds until the crackling dies down.

Add the cumin seeds and as soon as they change colour add the asafoetida.

Add the garlic, ginger, chopped onion, green chilli, shredded curry leaves and continue sautéing until the onions turn soft.

Add the turmeric, salt (to taste) and the potatoes. Cover tightly, reduce the heat and cook until the potatoes are cooked. Do not add any water, just allow the potatoes to cook in their own steam. They will cook well provided you do not keep the heat high.

Once potatoes are cooked add the green peas (if you like). If you are using fresh peas, cook them with the potato, if using frozen, add them once the potato is cooked.

Sprinkle the poha over the potatoes, add the lime juice, sugar, coconut and the chilli powder and cook until the poha turns soft.

Serve hot - immediately if possible - with half the coriander blended in and half sprinkled on top.

KOZHI PATTICE A LA VICTORIA

VICTORIA'S CHICKEN PATTIES

Makes 8–10

Simple potato cakes filled with spices and chicken mince are a very common part of the menu in many Parsee and Christian homes and were popular in Irani and Goan restaurants at one time. They are still popular in the small bars dotting 'older' Goa. The were traditionally made with leftover chicken, pork, beef or lamb. Victoria is the cook who visits two homes in my sister's building, cooking for both the families and we simply love her chicken patties, so this is her recipe.

Peel and cut the potatoes into thick slices wash well and keep soaking in water for 1–2 hours or, even, overnight.

Drain then boil the potatoes in fresh water for 6–10 minutes until just tender. Drain, return to the pan and dry, stirring with a wooden spatula, over a low heat. Mash well or pass through a ricer (ideally). Set aside.

Heat the oil in a large frying pan over a medium heat. Add the onions and sauté 3–4 minutes, until soft but not brown. Add the ginger, garlic and the ground spices. Stir then add the water and continue cooking until you can see the fat releasing, then add the tomato. Simmer until the tomato is pulpy.

Next stir in the mince and cook, stirring over a low heat until browned and all the grains are separated. Turn up the heat and sauté until the mince is cooked through and dry. Add the green chillies, coriander and mint, stir well and season to taste. Soak the bread slices in a little water and squeeze dry. Beat this well into the mashed potato and check the seasoning.

Divide the potato mixture into 8 or 10 equal-sized balls and divide the mince into the same number of portions.

Flatten a potato ball on the palm of your hand and spoon a portion of the mince in the middle, fold over the potato to encase the mince completely. Form into a thick cake. Repeat with the remaining portions of potato and mince.

Chill any leftover mince to serve another time.

Either griddle or shallow-fry the cakes until golden brown, about 3 minutes each side. You may dust with cornflour (cornstarch) before shallow-frying or, even, egg and breadcrumb them then deep-fry.

Parsees and Indian Catholics alike enjoy these with a mint yoghurt dressing or a dollop of tomato ketchup.

2–3 waxy potatoes

2–3 tbsp sunflower or rapeseed oil

4 red onions, finely chopped

5 cm (2 in) piece of fresh ginger,
very finely chopped

5–6 garlic cloves,
very finely chopped

1 tsp ground cumin

1⅓ tsp ground coriander

1 tsp chilli powder

½ tsp ground turmeric

100 ml (3½ fl oz/scant ½ cup) water

1–2 tomatoes, chopped

400 g–1 lb 2 oz minced
(ground) chicken

1–2 green chillies, seeds removed,
if liked, and very finely chopped

1 tbsp chopped coriander
(cilantro) leaves

1 sprig of mint, leaves picked
and chopped

2 white bread slices, crusts removed

oil for shallow-frying

salt to taste

To serve

mint yoghurt dressing
(see page 25)

400 g (14 oz/ scant 2 cups)
large sago pearls

1 small coconut, grated or (150 g (5 oz/
1²/₃ cups) desiccated coconut

150–200 g (1–1¹/₃ cups)
raw peanuts, without skins

2–3 tbsp ghee or rapeseed oil

2 tsp cumin seeds

2 pink or banana shallots,
very finely chopped

2 longish green chillies

5 cm (2 in) piece of fresh ginger

15–20 fresh curry leaves,
finely shredded

1 large floury potato, boiled,
peeled and diced

1 tsp caster (superfine) sugar

juice of ½ lime

salt to taste

a handful of chopped coriander
(cilantro) leaves

To serve

chapattis (see pages 183 or 185)
and chutney or cucumber raita

SABOODANA KHICHRI

SPICED SAGO WITH PEANUTS

Serves 4–6

This recipe I have to dedicate to Mr Bharat Boda of J P Boda and Co., who, sadly, is no longer around to enjoy this creation. He was one of our earliest guests and often asked me to make him this *Khichri* and I never obliged as I was too afraid to make it not having mastered it. It's too late to apologise but I hope you will enjoy making something so nourishing, unique and very tasty. Sago pearls are very commonly used across India and come in many forms. *Khichri* is a form of risotto and this is a great Indian classic, but hails from Maharashtra. I learned how to make it at a friend's house in Bombay, of course. It is an anytime of the day snack, meal, or just something to comfort you.

Wash the sago balls in a bowl in not too much water, swirl then drain and repeat until the water is clear. Then leave to soak in just enough water to cover for at least 3 hours or overnight.

If using desiccated coconut, soak in 150 ml (5fl oz/⅔ cup) water for 1 hour until soft and rehydrated and the water is absorbed.

Preheat the oven to 180°C/350°F/gas 4. Spread the peanuts out on a baking tray and toast until you get them lightly browned (about 15 minutes), stirring occasionally. Turn off the oven and leave inside until they become crunchy and toasted. Alternatively toss them in a dry frying pan over a medium heat until evenly golden then remove from the heat and leave until cold, stirring occasionally. Once toasted, crush coarsely in a clean coffee grinder or chop with a cleaver. A whirl or two in the grinder is often adequate but do not leave whole nuts.

Blend the crushed peanuts and coconut into the sago pearls and toss to mix well. Heat the oil in a deep, flameproof casserole or a wok with a lid, add the cumin seeds and cook for about 30 seconds until fragrant but not allowing them to burn. Add the shallots, green chillies and ginger and sauté for 3–4 minutes, or until the shallots are soft but not brown.

Stir in the curry leaves, then add the sago mixture. Mix well with a spatula, add the potato and mix well again. Reduce the heat, cover with a lid and let the khichri cook, gently stirring occasionally, until piping hot through.

Sprinkle over the sugar, lime juice and a little salt. Mix well, taste and re-season, if necessary.

Add plenty of chopped coriander, blend again taste and serve with the chapattis, chutney or raita – although I love it on its own.

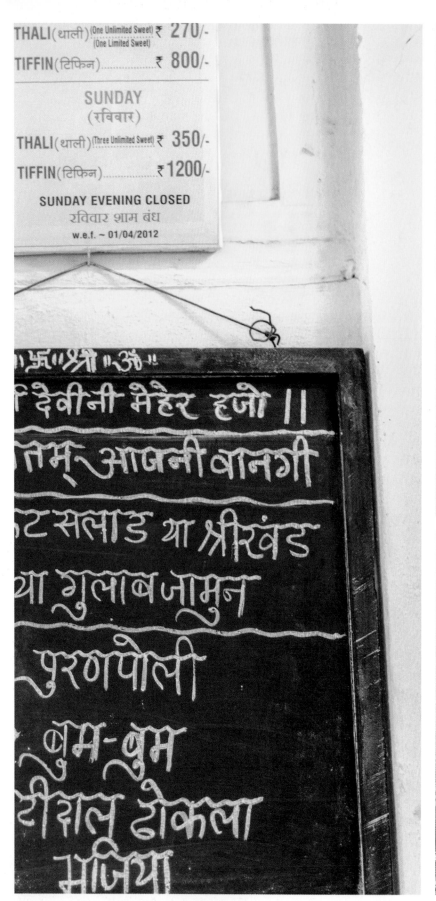

THALI (थाली) (One Unlimited Sweet) ₹ 270/-
(One Limited Sweet)
TIFFIN (टिफिन).......... ₹ 800/-

SUNDAY
(रविवार)

THALI (थाली) (Three Unlimited Sweet) ₹ 350/-

TIFFIN (टिफिन)......... ₹1200/-

SUNDAY EVENING CLOSED
रविवार शाम बंध
w.e.f. ~ 01/04/2012

ॐ "श्री" "ॐ"
दैवीनी मेहेर हजो ॥
ताम् आजनी वानगी
ट सलाड या श्रीखंड
या गुलाबजामुन
पुरणपोली
कुम-कुम
रीशालू ढोकला
भजिया

LUSAN MURCHA NA CHARVAELA EEDA

TODIWALA FAMILY'S MASALA SCRAMBLED EGGS

Serves 4

Like most Parsees, my family is egg-crazy and I, for one, can eat them every day (I particularly love bantam eggs, if you can get them). However, unlike others who will do many variations of scrambled eggs, this is our family recipe that we stick to and the one that we all love. We serve it with what we call Granu Toast in our extended family homes, but any good, crisp toast or crusty, hot rolls with oodles of butter would be great. Be very patient when cooking scrambled eggs of any sort. Have everything else ready – including the family drooling at the table – before you start cooking them!

Break the eggs into a bowl. Add the cream or milk and beat until well blended but not frothy. Set aside to rest.

Heat the oil in a smallish heavy-based non-stick saucepan or flameproof casserole, add the garlic and sauté until pale golden. Immediately add the butter and stir until melted. This will cool the pan down and not allow the garlic to over-colour.

Add the green chillies and sauté for another minute or two over a medium-low heat. Once the aroma is nearly tantalizing (the chillies do not need to cook well or brown so just softened is enough), make sure the heat is fairly low, then add the eggs. Use a wooden or plastic spatula (not a whisk) and stir very gently but continuously from side to side and edge to edge (eggs have a tendency to cook at the edge of the pan first and this will destroy your consistency if not gently stirred in all the time). Continue to stir slowly until rich and creamy and the egg is beginning to thicken and get lumpy. Do not allow the mixture to boil or it will curdle and spoil.

Remove the pan from the heat but keep stirring until you have a mottled yet lusciously creamy texture and the eggs are soft and runny but not watery and over cooked.

Add the chopped coriander.

Check for seasoning or leave the diners to adjust it for themselves. Serve with hot buttered toast and lots of everything else you may like.

8–10 eggs (depending on size)

2 tbsp single (light) cream or whole milk

1 tbsp sunflower or rapeseed oil

3–4 garlic cloves, very finely
chopped or minced

30 g (1 oz/2 tbsp) butter

2–3 slender green chillies, very finely
chopped or minced

1½ tbsp finely chopped coriander
(cilantro) leaves

salt to taste

To serve

hot toast and butter

KHAMAN DHOKLA

STEAMED LENTIL CAKES

Makes 24

This is a very popular snack item but is also eaten as part of a full Gujarati meal. The steamed chickpea cake pieces are drizzled with a sizzling mustard seed and curry leaf oil for added flavour. You can also add a tablespoon of buttermilk to the mix for extra fermentation. Some people use chickpea (garbanzo) flour but this is the traditional method. It may take a few attempts to master these, but patience will help you gain the experience to become an expert in cooking Indian food.

Put the split yellow peas or chickpeas in bowl. Add water to come about 2.5 cm (1 in) above the pulses. Cover with a clean cloth and leave to soak overnight. Do not refrigerate.

Purée in blender or food processor, but not too fine. Transfer to a bowl.

Beat well with a circular motion to incorporate air, either with a wooden spoon or a whisk. Leave to ferment for 5–6 hours.

Meanwhile, grind the ginger and green chillies together to a smooth paste in a mortar with a pestle (or a small bowl with the end of a rolling pin). Alternatively use a hand blender.

When the pea purée has fermented (it will rise a bit and smell fermented too), add half the oil, a little salt, the asafoetida, ground green chillies and ginger and beat well. Blend the bicarbonate of soda with the water and beat in.

Grease a 5 cm (2 in) deep baking dish or sandwich tin that will fit in a steamer with a little oil. Pour the mixture in it to about 2.5 cm (1 in) thickness.

Steam for 10–15 minutes or until risen and spongy and a knife inserted in the centre comes out clean.

Allow to cool slightly, but run a knife along the edges to release the steam. Cut into squares but do not remove from the dish.

Heat the remaining oil in a frying pan until a haze forms and add the mustard seeds. As the seeds crackle, add the curry leaves, toss and pour over the cakes, spreading it evenly over the top.

Serve garnished with as much coconut as you like and chopped coriander leaves. If using desiccated coconut, you may first like to soak it in 150 ml (5 fl oz/⅔ cup) water for an hour to rehydrate and become soft. Some also add a sprinkling of light sugar on the top. Serve with a tamaraind and date chutney or some Fresh Green Chutney.

250 g (9 oz/scant 1¼ cups)
yellow split peas or split
chickpeas (garbanzos)
2.5 cm (1 in) piece of fresh ginger
2–3 green chillies
50 ml (2 fl oz/¼ cup) sunflower
or rapeseed oil
salt to taste
pinch of ground asafoetida
½ tsp bicarbonate of soda
(baking soda)
2 tsp water
½ tsp black mustard seeds
1 sprig (10–12) fresh curry
leaves, shredded
150–300 g coconut, freshly
grated, or desiccated
(shredded) coconut
1 tbsp chopped coriander
(cilantro) leaves

To serve
tamarind and date chutney or
Fresh Green Chutney (see page 215)

6 green bananas or plantains

1 tsp ground turmeric

pinch of salt

3 floury potatoes, scrubbed

1½ tsp coriander seeds

1 tsp cumin seeds

2 onions, very finely chopped

4–6 garlic cloves, very finely
chopped or minced

2 green chillies, very finely
chopped or minced

1 heaped tbsp grated fresh ginger

2 tbsp chopped coriander
(cilantro) leaves

juice of 1 lime

about 150 g (5 oz/ 1¼ cups) plain
(all-purpose) flour

2–3 eggs

100 g (3½ oz/1¼ cups) fresh
breadcrumbs, or as required

oil for frying

To serve

tomato sauce (see page 29)
or a mayonnaise–based dip

KAERA NA CUTLESS

BANANA CUTLETS

Serves 4

This happens to be quite a classical dish in Parsee cuisine, though not cooked as often these days. These are simple yet tasty banana or plantain cakes, an ideal snack, starter or accompaniment to a main course.

Boil the bananas or plantains in their skins in water with the turmeric and the salt added for 15–20 minutes until tender when pierced with a knife. Drain and cool thoroughly before peeling.

Boil or steam the potatoes in their jackets, cool thoroughly then peel.

Gently roast the coriander and cumin seeds in a dry frying pan over a medium heat for about 30 seconds, stirring, until fragrant and slightly coloured.

Crush the seeds in a mortar with a pestle (or in a small bowl with the end of a rolling pin) to a coarse powder but ensure that no whole bits remain.

Mash the bananas with the potato and blend in the crushed seeds, onions, garlic, chillies, ginger, coriander and lime juice.

Work well to form a soft, yet dryish dough. Do not over-work as the potato may turn glue-like. Taste and re-season if necessary.

Divide into even-sized balls depending on the size you prefer. Make oblong or round shapes, dust with the flour, dip in beaten egg and then roll in breadcrumbs to coat completely.

Heat about 5 mm (¼ in) oil in a large frying pan or wok. Shallow-fry the cutlets turning once until crisp and golden, about 5 minutes. Serve with tomato sauce or a mayonnaise-based dip.

PAPETA PUR EEDU

EGGS ON POTATOES

Serves 4

A simple yet, funnily enough, variable egg recipe! My mother taught me this and, to date, she made the best I have ever had, including mine! This is, quite simply, divine. Parsees love eggs and an egg dish is a must at all celebrations if the host simply wishes to please the guests.

Good, soft old-fashioned bread with lots of good butter are also a must for the Parsee when eating eggs. If it's not heavenly – forget it!

Peel the potato and cut it into very thin slices, preferably using a mandoline or, otherwise, a large, sharp knife. Place in a bowl of cold water to prevent browning and set aside.

Heat the oil in a large frying pan, add the cumin seeds allow them to sizzle for a few seconds over a medium heat until just colouring. If using half oil half butter, just use the oil for frying the seeds then add the butter when coloured.

Add the chilli and garlic, sauté for a further minute or two then add the onion. Sauté for 2 minutes until softening but not browning, then pat dry the potato slices and add. Sauté for at least 3–4 minutes, sprinkle with a little salt and then spread out evenly in the pan.

Add enough water to come just below the level of the contents, bring to the boil, reduce the heat to low, cover and cook until the potatoes are just tender when pierced with a knife, but still hold their shape. The time will depend on the potatoes used so check them often.

At this stage I like to sprinkle the dish with the spring onion, but it is optional.

Sprinkle the coriander over, mix gently by folding the contents in a slow motion, taste and re-season if necessary then level out again. Ensure that the sides of the pan are clean.

Make 4 indentations evenly spaced around the potato cake about 4 cm (1½ in) in from the edge. Break an egg into each cavity. Cover the pan and cook over a very low heat until cooked to your liking (I prefer my yolk soft). Cut the cake into quarters ensuring each portion has an egg in it and serve with mango chutney and soft bread.

1 large waxy potato

2–3 tbsp sunflower or rapeseed oil
(or half butter and half oil)

1 tsp cumin seeds

1 small green chilli, finely chopped

2 garlic cloves, finely chopped

1 onion, thinly sliced

salt to taste

1 small spring onion (scallion),
thinly sliced (optional)

4 eggs

1 heaped tbsp finely chopped
coriander (cilantro)

To serve
mango chutney and soft bread

SEAFOOD & FISH

Several countries in the world have large coastlines and India has its fair share of a vast coastline – its waters inhabited by a wonderful array of amazing seafood. Nature's marine bounty is celebrated by thousands of dishes spanning north to south, east to west. The sub continent possesses a vibrant bounty from its many rivers too and, in the North of India in particular (and in Bengal of course), it is river fish that hold sway in their cuisine with very little appreciation for marine species.

Bombay is the place of the veritable bommelo or bombil affectionately known as Bombay duck! But besides that it boasts a fabulous catch and you will often now see restaurants specialising in coastal recipes of Bombay's coastal bounty from fabulous fish to jumbo prawns, crabs, rock lobsters, clams and mussels, squid and cuttlefish.

The coastal cuisine changes rapidly from north to south and east to west. From simple fish frying or grilling in banana leaves in Gujarat to the coconut-influenced dishes of Maharashtra, Goa, Karnataka and Kerala and along the east coast until you reach Bengal (where fish is a passion), having no fish would be the end of the world. Likewise, just as in Goa, fish curry and rice is a daily staple and it would be a sad world to live in if that was taken away.

My wife Pervin and I were extremely fortunate in having the opportunity to go to the fish market with our dads when we were young. Though at different ends of town! Dad was a great fish bargainer! And on Sunday mornings I would accompany him to the market to buy the week's supply of meat, fish poultry and vegetables. The knowledge I gained about how to select fresh from made-to-look fresh produce was invaluable to me, and my love for freshness and variety grows. Sunday was the day for feasting and all our favourite foods, which was often fish, were cooked on Sunday afternoons. My father-in-law on the other had was a confirmed shopaholic and would buy excessive amounts of anything he fancied, thereby coming home to often face criticism from my mother-in-law who would be fear-struck with the huge purchases. To him, anything new had to be tried, much to his family's disgust as they ended up cleaning the fish and cooking it.

Bombay Fish Markets are exciting places to be. Traditionally only the women sell fish within the Koli – fisher folk community men don't sell fish as it's taboo and folklore dictates that they do not know how to make money, so it's the women who dominate the market vending scene, overlooked by cats and crows.

I hope you enjoy these recipes and explore the seafood available locally to you. It is the under-utilised and sustainable seafood that we need to explore. Due to traditional promotion of just a few fish we have lost our love for others, which is not only wrong, it endangers the stocks of the more common varieties. So please do be daring and try something different the next time you cook with fish. You will be supporting our depleting fishing fleets and generations of family businesses and professions.

For the masala

5–6 whole red chillies (kashmiri are best)

5–6 garlic cloves

5 cm (2 in) piece of fresh ginger

5 cm (2 in) piece of cinnamon stick

3 green cardamom pods, split

3–4 cloves

1 tbsp coriander seeds

1 heaped tsp cumin seeds

5–6 black peppercorns

250 ml (8½ fl oz/1 cup) palm
   or cider vinegar

2 smallish sea bass or other
   smallish whole fish (see recipe intro),
   about 250 g (9 oz) each

1 tsp ground turmeric

1 tbsp lime juice

1 tsp salt or to taste

2 tbsp sunflower or rapeseed oil

8–10 curry leaves (preferably fresh)

1 onion, finely chopped

2 tomatoes, chopped

To serve

sliced deep-fried potatoes, grilled tomato
   slices and salad

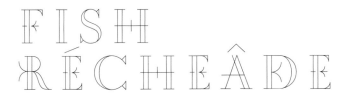

FISH RÉCHEÂDE

GOAN-STYLE STUFFED FISH

Serves 2

Récheâde is a cooking style typical of Goa and comes from the Portuguese, *recheado* meaning stuffed. Sea bass or Pomfret (pompano) are the favourite types of fish to use for this dish but smallish mackerel or grey mullet are just as good. There are many variations to *Récheâde* but this one does work extremely well.

For the masala, place the chillies, garlic, ginger, cinnamon, cardamom, cloves, coriander seeds, cumin, peppercorns and vinegar in a blender or small food processor and grind to a smooth paste. Alternatively, use a mortar with a pestle (or small bowl with the end of a rolling pin) to grind the spices then work in the vinegar. Set aside.

Clean the tiny scales from the body of the sea bass and remove the fins. You will find that there are tiny scales below the fin area too and these will need removing (if you use mackerel, they won't need descaling).

Using a sharp knife, cut along the back of the fish, from head to tail. Continue cutting into the fish, easing the flesh away from the bones. Work gradually until you come to the abdominal cavity but don't cut through the skin. Make sure that you get the flesh off the bones as cleanly as possible. The best way to achieve this is to keep the blade of the knife tilted towards the bones and not towards the flesh. Turn the fish over and cut down the other side of the backbone from tail to head, easing the flesh away as before.

Snip the backbone with scissors at the head and tail end and remove it. Pull out the entrails, rinse out the cavity and pat dry with paper towels. Feel along the flesh inside and remove any loose bones too, ideally with tweezers or with the fingers.

Repeat with the second fish.

Blend together the turmeric, lime juice and half the salt and rub this inside the fish.

Heat the oil in a frying pan. Add the curry leaves and onion and sauté for about 3 minutes over a high heat until golden. Add the masala and cook until the oil runs then stir in the tomatoes.

Cook for a few minutes and season. Remove from the heat and cool slightly.

Spread the mixture into the fish. Some people prefer to tie the fish lightly so that the filling does not come out. However if you are careful very little will come out anyway.

Heat a little oil in a large frying pan. Fry the fish gently for 3–4 minutes each side until golden and cooked through. You can also finish the fish in a hot oven in a baking dish after sautéeing it on either side first. Serve with sliced deep-fried potatoes, grilled tomato slices and salad.

3–4 tbsp sunflower or rapeseed oil

4 small red onions, finely chopped

6 garlic cloves, crushed

7.5–10 cm (3.5–4 in) piece of fresh ginger, finely chopped or grated

3 pomfrets (pompano) each trimmed and cut into 2.5 cm (1 in) thick steaks through the bone or filleted (alternatively use sea bass, turbot, or halibut steaks)

15-20 fresh curry leaves, finely shredded

1 litre (34 fl oz/4¼ cups) water

8 cherry tomatoes, halved

6 eggs

60 g (2 oz/⅓ cup) fine grade rice flour

90–120 ml (3–4 fl oz/⅓ – ½ cup) malt vinegar

85–115 g (3–4 oz/⅓ – ½ cup) caster (superfine) sugar

1 bunch coriander (cilantro), finely chopped

3 sprigs of mint, leaves picked and chopped

4 tsp ground cumin

4–5 medium green chillies, finely chopped

salt to taste

To serve

chapattis (see pages 183 or 185) or khichdi (see page 200)

SAAS NI MACCHI

PARSEE FISH IN WHITE SAUCE

Serves 4–6

Saas simply means 'sauce', however I am not sure
whether this was the Parsee take on their fish
velouté but it is a velouté of sorts except that it is
thickened with eggs and ground rice instead of flour
and butter. The flavouring is very Parsee and this
dish is very much a signature of the community and
a must at most special occasions.

Pomfret (pompano) is the most popular fish to
use. It's a meaty flat fish from the Arabian Sea much
prized by the people of the west coast of India and
coastal Pakistan. Pomfret is also found in the Indian
Ocean but somehow the taste is just not the same.
You can use any good white chunky fish fillet, like
sea bass, turbot, halibut or, even coley, but ideally
use one that can be cut into steaks with a central
bone (you could use four cod cutlets, for instance)
so that the fish can be simmered in the sauce itself.

Heat the oil in a flameproof casserole and sauté the onions, garlic and ginger until
just beginning to colour.

Add the fish and shredded curry leaves and fry on each side for 1 minute.

Add the water and tomatoes, bring to the boil, reduce the heat and simmer
gently for a few minutes until fish is just cooked through (steaks will take a
little longer than fillets). Remove the fish with a fish slice and place in a deep dish.
Keep warm. Strain the stock, return to the casserole and reheat it.

Beat the eggs with the rice flour, vinegar, sugar, coriander and mint until smooth.
Whisk the hot fish stock into the egg mixture and then pour back into the pan.
Cook, stirring slowly but continuously, until it thickens. Do not let it boil (best to
use a wooden flat spatula and a whisk alternately to achieve this and to prevent the
egg from curdling).

Whisk in the cumin and, once well blended, the chopped green chillies. Season
with salt and check that you are happy with the sweet, sour and slightly hot tastes.

Either add the fish to the sauce (if using steaks with bone in) and heat through,
or pour the sauce over the fish (if using fillets).

Serve immediately with chapattis or khichdi.

MASALA MA TARAELI MACHCHI

PARSEE-STYLE FRIED FISH

Serves 4

This is a classic Parsee fish marinated in a simple
masala and shallow fried. I love to serve it with my
all-time favourite, *dhan daar nay vaghar*, which is
cooked, puréed lentils sizzled with garlic and cumin
and served with deep-fried crisp onions as well as
the rice. Pomfret (pompano) is the favourite fish
in India but sea bass, plaice, tilapia or, even, coley
is fine. Dust the marinated fillets in flour, coat in
beaten egg, then semolina or coarse-ground rice
instead of breadcrumbs. Deep-fry until crisp and
golden. Both styles produce great results.

Rub salt and turmeric into the fillets and set aside for 30 minutes.

Make a paste with the remaining ingredients except the oil. Taste the paste
and check for seasoning. If you like more lime juice or salt, go ahead and add.

Spread the paste over the fish and either cook straight away or cover well
and leave to marinate in the refrigerator for a few hours or overnight, if liked
(the marinade may cure the fish to a degree so less cooking time will be required).

Heat enough oil to cover the base of a large frying pan over a medium heat and
fry the fish gently until browned well underneath before carefully turning it over
to cook the other sides. Do not make the pan too hot, as the masala will burn very
rapidly. When ready the fish should be crisp on the outside and delicately soft
on the inside.

Drain on paper towels, if necessary, and serve with tomatoes, fresh lime and
sliced fried potatoes. Alternatively, you can also dust the fish lightly in rice before
adding to the pan.

8 small pieces of white fish fillet, each
about 10 cm (4 in) long

salt to taste

¼ tsp ground turmeric

1 tbsp lime or lemon juice

1 tsp medium-hot chilli powder

1 tsp ground cumin

salt to taste

1½ tsp ground coriander

1 tsp ginger and garlic paste
(see page 157), or use
1 large garlic clove, crushed and ¾ tsp
grated fresh ginger

oil for frying

To serve
tomatoes, wedges of lime and
sliced fried potatoes

500 g (1 lb 2 oz) firm white fish, filleted
and cut into large chunks
(we use pomfret (pompano) but coley,
cod or tilapia are good)

For the masala
100 g (3½ oz) fat red chillies
1 tbsp coriander seeds
1½ tsp cumin seeds
6–8 garlic cloves
4 cm (1½ in) piece of fresh ginger
½ tsp ground turmeric
1 medium-sized coconut, grated, or 200 g
(7 oz/2¼ cups) desiccated
(shredded) coconut

50 g (2 oz) piece of tamarind block
100 ml (3½ fl oz/scant ½ cup)
hot water
salt to taste
a pinch of ground turmeric
about 75 ml (2½ fl oz/ ⅓ cup) sunflower
or rapeseed oil
1 onion, halved and finely sliced
2.5 cm (1 in) piece fresh ginger, grated
2 green chillies, finely shredded
300 ml (10 fl oz/1¼ cups) fish
or chicken stock, or water
2–3 kokum or 1 sour plum
(or 1 tbsp lime juice)

To serve
curry rice and kachumber (see page 93)

XIT ANI NISHTYA CHI KODI

GOAN FISH CURRY

Serves 4

Fish curry is synonymous with Goa. It is a staple
part of the daily diet and a vast majority of
Goans cannot do without it. Instead of white fish,
you can add crab or lobster meat, shelled prawns,
mussels or, even, oysters. For a veggie option,
add cauliflower, tomatoes and par-boiled baby
potatoes (cook in the sauce until tender). It is
not suitable for red meat but is good with chicken
(sauté for about 5 minutes first until browned and
almost cooked through before adding to the sauce).

Grind the masala ingredients with a little water in a blender or food processor to a
smooth thick paste. Add water a little at a time and ensure that it does not become
too runny (you will need more if using desiccated coconut rather than fresh). You
can also smoothen the paste by pressing it through a sieve or strainer.

Soak the tamarind in the hot water for 1 hour. Mix well with the hands then rub
the mixture through a sieve into a bowl.

Rinse and dry the fish on paper towels. Sprinkle with a little salt and the turmeric
and set aside. Heat enough oil to cover the base of a flameproof casserole dish.
When the oil forms a haze, add the onion, ginger and green chillies. Sauté for
3 minutes then add in the masala paste. Sauté until the oil begins to run again
(this shows the masala is cooked). Stir regularly to prevent sticking. Add the stock
or water and bring to the boil. Reduce the heat and add the tamarind pulp and the
kokum or sour plum (or lime juice) to taste.

Simmer for 5 minutes or so and check the seasoning. Check the consistency and
ensure that it is not too thin but more like a pouring sauce. Simmer a little longer,
if necessary.

Add the fish in and continue simmering without stirring for 5 minutes over a
medium heat. Bring to the boil and remove from the heat. Cover and leave to stand
for 5 minutes to finish cooking the fish, giving it the perfect texture. Remove the
kokum or sour plum, if liked, and serve with steamed curry rice and kachumber.

KOLMI NO PATIO

PRAWNS IN HOT & SWEET SAUCE

Serves 4

This is a much simplified version of the traditional Parsee prawn patia, which is normally served as a pickle accompaniment to my favourite lentil dish, *dhaan daar* (simply puréed cooked lentils, sizzled with garlic and cumin and served with deep-fried crisp onions) but it can also enjoyed on its own with fresh, hot chapattis (see pages 183 or 185). Patio is a classical dish and it is rare to find this version on sale anywhere. Most restaurants do not know that a classical recipe exists and make something bright red in colour, which is not authentic.

Devein and wash the prawns, toss in the lemon juice and turmeric and set aside.

Heat 2–3 tablespoons of the oil in a flameproof casserole and add the curry leaves and aubergine. Sauté until well browned then remove with a slotted spoon and set aside.

Next add a tablespoon more oil and sauté the squash until browning slightly. Remove and repeat with more oil and the onions. Sauté until golden brown, then add the green chilli, chilli powder, ground coriander, cumin and the ginger and garlic paste.

Sauté for 2–3 minutes over a medium-low heat and add the chopped tomatoes. Cook, stirring, for a further 2–3 minutes and add the tamarind and jaggery.

Stir until the tamarind and jaggery are fully dissolved, then add the aubergine and squash and check for seasoning.

The Patio needs to be a little hot, sweet and sour.

Finally add the prawns and cook for 2–3 minutes or until the prawns are pink. If you are storing the Patio as a pickle, use a little extra oil and cook the prawns a little longer so that no fresh prawn moisture remains and the Patio looks like a thick pickle. Garnish with a sprinkling of fresh coriander and salt. Serve with chapattis or some hot daal and steamed rice.

500 g (1 lb 2 oz) raw, peeled prawns

juice of ½ lemon

1 tsp ground turmeric

4–6 tbsp sunflower or
rapeseed oil

10–12 curry leaves, preferably fresh

1 aubergine (eggplant), diced

150–200 g (5–7 oz) red kuri (or other
winter squash) flesh, diced

2 onions, finely chopped

1 green chilli, seeded and chopped

1 heaped tsp chilli powder

1 tbsp ground coriander

1 heaped tbsp ground cumin

2 tbsp ginger and garlic paste
(see page 157),
or use 5–6 garlic cloves, crushed
and 1 tbsp grated fresh ginger

2 large tomatoes, chopped

2–3 tbsp fresh tamarind pulp
(or 1 tbsp tamarind paste)

100 g (3½ oz/scant ½ cup) jaggery
(or muscovado sugar)

To serve

2 tbsp chopped coriander (cilantro) leaves

salt to taste (optional)

chapattis (see pages 183 or 185)

or Boiled Rice (see page 195)

or daal (see page 133)

3 whole pomfrets (pompano), or use plaice other plump flat fish or even seabass, cut in 2.5 cm (1 in) thick steaks, through the bone

salt to taste

½ tsp ground turmeric

banana leaves, as required

a little malt vinegar for steaming

For the chutney

1 coconut, grated, or 200g (7 oz/2¼ cups) desiccated (shredded) coconut

1 large bunch of coriander (cilantro)

4–5 green chillies

6–8 garlic cloves

1 heaped tsp cumin seeds

1 tbsp caster (superfine) sugar

juice of 1 large lime or a small lemon

1 large bunch of mint

PATRANI MACCHI

STEAMED FISH IN BANANA LEAF

Serves 4–6

This is a classical Parsee fish preparation and is very popular at weddings and other festive occasions. Banana leaves are available in some Asian stores. Alternatively, use squares of oiled foil or double-thickness greaseproof paper. You can also use the chutney to spread over fillets or whole fish before grilling (broiling). Use the large bunches of herbs available in Asian stores and markets, not little bags from a supermarket.

Rub each slice of fish with a little salt and the turmeric and set aside whilst you proceed with the chutney.

If using desiccated coconut, mix it with 150 ml (5 fl oz/²/₃ cup) water and leave to soak for 1 hour until soft and rehydrated and the liquid is absorbed. Grind the coconut with all the remaining chutney ingredients in a food processor to a thick paste, adding a little more water if necessary. Do not use too much though, the mixture must not be too runny. Stop and scrape down the sides as necessary and re-start until smooth.

Coat each slice of fish with the coconut chutney on either side.

Remove the stems on the banana leaves and trim the sides. Cut them into squares big enough to wrap each fish piece. The leaves have to be warmed to make them soft and supple. To do this just run them over the burner or hot plate and you will see it change colour and become soft. Do not overdo it, just one pass on either side is often sufficient. Take care not to burn your hands. Alternatively, heat a dry frying pan and flip them in the hot pan for a second or two. Wipe the leaves before you do this.

Wrap each piece of coated fish in a piece of banana leaf. Tie with string or wrap firmly, keeping the folded side at the bottom to prevent the chutney from coming out.

Place the fish in a steamer over a pan of simmering water, sprinkled with vinegar, cover and steam for 20 minutes until the fish is cooked or preheat the oven to 190°C/375°F/gas 5. Place the wrapped fish in a shallow baking tin, sprinkle some vinegar and a little water over the parcels and bake for 20 minutes. Transfer to serving plates and remove the string if tied. The fish is served in the banana leaf.

BADA JHINGA CHUTT PUTTA

HOT & SPICY TIGER PRAWNS

Serves 4

A hot yet delectable masala that is ideal for king prawns, lobsters, crab and the like for grilling directly over a barbecue or chargrill, in a tandoor, or under a grill (broiler).

You may wish to remove the heads from the prawns first, but the head cooks well, tastes very good and helps prevent too much shrinkage. Butterfly the prawns by slitting down the back of the shell, with a small, sharp knife, not quite right through the flesh and opening up. Remove the black vein that runs down the length of the body.

Wash the prawns and dry on paper towels. Mix the turmeric with half the lime juice and rub it into the split prawns.

Remove the stems from the chillies and put them in a blender or small food processor. Add the remaining marinade ingredients and purée to a fine paste. Taste for seasoning. The marinade should be hot and tangy.

Spread the marinade all over the prawns. place them in a covered container and marinate in the refrigerator for several hours.

When cooking the prawns directly over a chargrill or barbecue the heat should be high to seal fast, but not intense. If too hot, the prawns will char and the marinade will not cook well.

Brown the prawns shell side up first for a couple of minutes, turn over and cook until cooked through and bright pinky-red. If the heat is perfect the prawns should not take more than 5–6 minutes to cook.

Peel and enjoy.

12–16 large whole king prawns

1 tsp ground turmeric

1½ tbsp lime juice

For the marinade

8–10 large red chillies

1½ tbsp lime juice

8–10 garlic cloves

5 cm (2 in) piece of fresh ginger

1 tsp cumin seeds

1 heaped tsp coriander seeds

12–15 black peppercorns

2 tbsp fresh tamarind pulp

(see page 59)

salt to taste

2 tbsp sunflower or rapeseed oil, plus

extra for cooking

MEAT & POULTRY

I do get confronted many times as an Indian by know-it-all people relating to meat-eating in India.

'You don't eat Venison in India!' Yes we do, and have been for centuries. In fact it is also a myth that all Hindus are vegetarians and do not eat meat. According to legend, the God Rama and his brother Laxmana and his wife Sita, were exiled from their kingdom and lived in the forest for several years. During this time Laxman, best bowman of his era, would hunt for deer daily for their meals. That is proof in itself!

'Indians do not eat pork.' Yes, some of us do. We have all types of people living in our country and for some, such as the people of Assam, pork is a regular meat, so also in Goa with the Catholic community, likewise the Christians. However the Assamese are Hindus and one must also know that Vasco da Gama was motivated to settle in Goa rather than in Kerala, where they first set base, because he saw the local Hindus eat pork whenever they celebrated. The Hindus of Goa largely do not eat pork now, but they did a few hundred years ago.

'Your people do not eat beef.' We eat beef too, but the cow is sacred and hence cannot be slaughtered. You often see stray cows in cities and towns because once old the owner can no longer afford to look after them or feed them, and since they cannot be slaughtered, it is better that they be let loose to fend for themselves. Bulls are allowed to be slaughtered as is the Indian water buffalo, which is also sold as beef.

'Game would never be found on an Indian menu.' Game is or was commonly eaten in rural regions and I was privileged to grow up in a household where we often ate partridge, grouse, buck, blue bull, geese and ducks in season and wild boar, and these feature on menus in my restaurants.

'Indians would never cook with lamb or goat.' Regardless of which animal it is, both are called mutton in India and this term is not related to the age of the animal or the sex. Mostly goat is consumed, though sheep are also bred and in Hindi they are known as *bhaed* (though that may not be evident when sold as meat).

We have poultry too and chicken is the most commonly eaten of them all. Duck is popular in Kerala and in some other parts and during the migratory season hunters all over the country will be out in the fields shooting ducks and geese. Chicken is of course widely farmed and the days of eating mostly free-range organic chicken have long since come to pass.

All I say is that we must buy good meat. We must know where it came from and how it was reared. Animal welfare should be at the top of our agenda and hence we should demand the best and often local produce, wherever you are, is best.

POUSSINS PERI-PERI

CHICKEN COOKED THE HOT GOAN/PORTUGUESE WAY

Serves 4

The peri-peri chicken of Goa is named after the Piri-Piri or bird's eye chilli, brought to Goa by the Portuguese from South America. They also planted it in Mozambique and Angola and it now thrives in many parts of Africa. The Goans, however, changed the style of the original peri-peri chicken which was simply cooked in a paste of crumbled red chillies, lime juice and lots of garlic. To make a traditional Indian peri-peri paste is very time consuming, so here is a simplified recipe which would be to a Goan absolute taboo ... but it works!

The same chilli is also the base for the famed Goan Pork Vindaloo, derived from another Portuguese dish of meat and wine (which evolved into vinegar and then the spices, including the fiery chillies, added).

Wipe the poussins inside and out with paper towels and make three or four slashes on the breasts on each side of the breast bone so they form 'V' shapes along it . Make a few slashes on the legs and thighs too.

Mix the turmeric and lime juice together and rub it well into the poussins. Chill in the refrigerator for about an hour.

Meanwhile, mix all the masala ingredients together to form a paste and taste for seasoning. If you find it too mild add more chilli powder.

Rub the masala well into the poussins on all sides and leave to marinate in the refrigerator for at least 2 hours or, if possible, overnight.

Before cooking the poussins, prepare the roasting dish. Grease a large ovenproof frying pan with a little olive oil and lay the thickly sliced tomato in a single layer. Drizzle with more olive oil on the top too, sprinkle liberally with salt and pepper.

Preheat the oven to 180°C/350°F/gas 4. Place the poussins in a roasting tin right-side up and, if not sitting straight, press down firmly on the legs. The birds will take on a plump look and sit perfectly. Place them in the oven and after 10 minutes reduce the temperature to 150°C/300°F/gas 2.

After 30 minutes remove the poussins from the oven. Carefully lift out the poussins onto a plate. Spread the onion and potatoes evenly in the roasting tin. Put the poussins back on top and return to the oven.

After about 10 minutes place the frying pan with the tomatoes over a high heat and let the tomato slices brown on the bottom. Do not flip over but just lift to check that the slices are browning. Transfer the pan to the top shelf of the oven. Remove the poussins and turn them over breast-side down on the onion and potato and place back in the oven. Check to see if potatoes are almost tender. If so, after 2 minutes, switch off the oven and let it all rest in the oven for a good 10 minutes.

Carefully lift out the poussins and cut in halves. Mix the onions and potatoes, check the seasoning and plate in a separate dish. Serve the chicken along with the potatoes and onions, the pan of tomatoes, a mixed salad and some crusty bread.

For the chicken

2 oven-ready poussins (spring chicken)

1 tsp ground turmeric

juice of 1 lime

For the masala

1½ heaped tbsp chilli powder

1 heaped tbsp ginger and garlic paste

(see page 157) (or use

3 garlic cloves crushed and

2 tsp grated fresh ginger)

1 tsp garam masala

1 tsp ground cumin

2 tsp ground coriander

2 tbsp cider (apple cider) vinegar

1 tsp salt

3 tbsp olive oil

2 large beef tomatoes,

cut in 1 cm (½ in) thick slices

olive oil

salt (preferably sea salt) and freshly

ground black pepper

2 red onions, sliced into rings

3 potatoes, thickly sliced

To serve

mixed salad and crusty bread

1 tsp cumin seeds

1 tbsp coriander seeds

250 ml (8 ½ fl oz/1 cup) hot water

2 thin green chillies, roughly chopped

5–6 garlic cloves

5 cm (2 in) piece of fresh ginger,
  roughly chopped

2 tbsp rapeseed oil

7.5 cm (3 in) piece of cinnamon stick

3–4 green cardamom pods, split

3–4 cloves

2–3 dried whole red chillies

2 onions, finely chopped

½ tsp ground turmeric powder

1 tsp chilli powder

500 g (1 lb 2 oz) lean minced
  (ground) lamb

2–3 tomatoes, chopped

sea salt and freshly ground pepper

2 heaped tbsp chopped
  coriander (cilantro) leaves

1 sprig of mint, leaves picked
  and shredded

3–4 waxy potatoes, boiled and
  diced (optional)

4 eggs

To serve

chapattis (see pages 183 or 185)

KHEEMA PUR EEDU

SPICED MINCE TOPPED WITH CODDLED OR FRIED EGG

Serves 4

Mince of all types, when cooked with the right balance of spices and condiments, gives a meal full of beautiful flavours and aromas and is highly versatile with many different ways of serving. Here we bring to you a simple Parsee-style lamb mince which can be served with a fried egg on top, or scrambled with egg, or baked with egg, or served with the Parsee favourite, Sali, crisp straw potatoes. You could use bought crisp potato sticks and simply heat them briefly in the oven.

Gently toast the cumin and coriander seeds in a dry frying pan until lightly coloured and fragrant (about 30 seconds). Soak in the hot water with the green chillies, garlic and ginger. When the seeds have puffed up, purée the mixture to a smooth paste in a blender or small food processor. If not smooth, pass through a sieve (strainer) and try puréeing again or finish in a mortar and pestle.

Heat the oil in a flameproof casserole and sauté the cinnamon, cardamom, cloves and whole red chillies over a medium heat until the cloves are slightly swollen. Add the onions and sauté until browned, about 5 minutes.

Add the paste, turmeric and chilli powder and sauté, stirring well from the bottom, until the oil seeps out.

Remove from the heat and allow to cool a little and then beat in the mince to break up all the lumps. Add a little more water to slacken the mixture then return to the heat stirring well for the first few minutes. Continue to cook making sure no lumps form and, when cooked through, add the tomatoes. Continue simmering until most of the liquid has evaporated but everything is tender and moist.

Season to taste and add the chopped coriander and mint and, if serving the Parsee way, then stir in the diced potatoes and heat through. It can be served just like this, but to serve with the eggs, spread the cooked mince out in a baking dish and remove the cinnamon stick, cardamom pods and cloves.

Preheat the oven to 120°C/240°F/gas ½.

Make 4 indentations at intervals round the dish and break an egg into each. Cover the dish with foil. Place the dish in a large baking tin with enough boiling water to come half way up the sides of the dish. Bake in the oven for about 20 minutes or until the eggs are cooked to your liking. The best is to have a luxurious creamy buttery yolk and soft whites.

An alternative method is to flatten the mince in the casserole dish make the 4 indentations, break in the eggs, cover and cook over a gentle heat until the eggs set (about 10 minutes or longer if you like them firm). Serve with warm chapattis.

CHICKEN KEBAB. Rs 160/DZ.

MUTTON KEBAB Rs 160/DZ.

For the masala

6–8 dried red chillies

1½ tsp cumin seeds

1½ tbsp coriander seeds

2.5 cm (1 in) piece of cinnamon stick

4–5 green cardamom pods, split

4–5 cloves

For the chicken

200 g (7 oz) dried apricots (unbleached
   and organic)

250 ml (8½ fl oz/1 cup) hot water

4 tbsp sunflower or rapeseed oil

2 x 2.5 cm (1 in) pieces of cinnamon stick

2 onions, chopped

2 heaped tbsp garlic and ginger paste
   (see page 157) or use 6 garlic cloves,
   crushed and 1 heaped tbsp grated
   fresh ginger

500–600 g (1 lb 2 oz–1 lb 5 oz) boneless
   chicken, cut into 2 cm (¾ in) dice

salt to taste

4 tomatoes, chopped

1–2 tbsp chopped coriander (cilantro) leaves

To serve

Sali (crisp straw potatoes)

bread or chapattis (see pages 183 or 185) or
   Boiled Rice (see page 195)

JARDALOO MA MURGHI
CHICKEN WITH APRICOTS

Serves 4

This sounds very basic but it is a very popular Parsee chicken dish served at festive occasions, weddings etc. The Parsee tradition of cooking with dry and fresh fruits dates back to our ancestry from Persia. The Persians, incidentally, were the first to establish cooking as an art as well as turn it into a culinary form. The apricots used here come from India or Pakistan and have a stone which, when cracked, yields a tasty nut. You can find them in Indian food stores. They taste richer and less tart than other dried apricots. We Parsees would garnish this with Sali – crisp straw potatoes. You could buy crisp potato sticks and heat them briefly in the oven.

Grind the masala ingredients in a clean coffee grinder, small food processor, mortar with a pestle or in a small bowl with the end of a rolling pin. Set aside.

Soak the apricots in the water for 2–3 hours (or overnight if more convenient) until soft and swollen. The Indian apricots will have a stone inside, which you may like to remove before putting them into the gravy. We do not do so at home, instead we put them on the side when we eat the meal and then crack and eat them later. If you do remove the stones, they may lose their texture and pulp into the sauce.

When ready to cook the chicken, heat the oil in a heavy-based pan until hazy and add the cinnamon sticks. When they have absorbed some of the oil and puffed a bit – about 1½ minutes – add the onions and brown slowly.

When the onions are browned add the ginger and garlic and the prepared masala and sauté well until the oil, which has been absorbed, is released slowly around the edges of the onions.

Add the chicken and sauté for 4–5 minutes or until half done. Add a little salt, the chopped tomatoes and the soaked apricots and any residual soaking water, mix well, cover and simmer until the chicken is tender, about 30 minutes.

If the sauce is too thin, uncover and cook for a few minutes until rich and thick but take care not to overcook the chicken. If really necessary, remove the chicken with a slotted spoon before boiling the sauce rapidly to thicken and reduce, then return the chicken to the pan.

Stir in the chopped coriander, taste and re-season, if necessary. Sprinkle with the straw potatoes and serve with bread or chapattis, or boiled rice.

6–8 large chicken leg portions, cut in two
    at the thigh joint 200 g (7 oz/1⅓ cups)

For the first masala

200 g (7 oz/1⅓ cups) raw cashew nuts

3 tbsp sunflower or rapeseed oil

1 tsp cumin seeds

1 heaped tbsp butter

2 red or white onions, sliced

7.5 cm (3 in) piece of fresh ginger,
    finely chopped

6–8 garlic cloves

1 heaped tbsp ground almonds

1 heaped tbsp coconut milk powder

1–2 longish green chillies, seeded, if liked

For the second masala

2 tbsp sunflower or rapeseed oil

7.5 cm (3 in) piece of cinnamon stick,
    broken in two

3–4 green cardamom pods, split

2–3 cloves

2 large kashmiri dried red chillies,
    broken into pieces and seeded

1–2 green chillies, quartered lengthways

500 ml (17 fl oz/2¼ cups) water

8–10 cherry tomatoes, halved

salt to taste

6 potatoes, each peeled
    and cut into 3–4 pieces

oil for deep-frying

KAJU NI MURGHI

CHICKEN WITH CASHEW NUTS

Serves 6

Parsee cuisine has amalgamated with the broader Indian cuisine but it still has several links with its Persian roots. Although we love to eat and enjoy life, rich food is seldom cooked in the house, but we do indulge on special occasions! This chicken dish is a simplified version of the original and may not be as rich as it used to be but, these days, with little time for cooking, it would be too complicated. It is best enjoyed with crisp chunks of deep-fried crisp potatoes and chapattis.

Wipe the chicken with paper towels. Set aside.

Soak the cashew nut pieces in hot water for 1–2 hours until soft. If using whole cashew nuts, roughly chop before soaking. Drain and reserve the water in a measuring jug and make up to 300–400 ml (10–13 fl oz/1¼ –1¾ cups) with fresh water. Set aside.

Heat the oil in a pan and sauté the chicken pieces, skin side down and then turn over and brown the other sides. Remove from the pan and drain on paper towels. Add the cumin seeds to the same oil and sauté for a few seconds until fragrant then add butter and, when foaming, add the onions. Sauté over a medium–low heat until the onions are soft but not brown, about 4 minutes. Remove from the heat and leave to cool.

Purée the onions and remaining first masala ingredients together in a blender with the measured nut water until smooth. If necessary pass through a sieve (strainer), and set aside.

Heat the oil in a deep flameproof casserole and, when a haze forms, add the cinnamon, cardamom seeds and cloves, stirring until the cloves swell and all is fragrant. Reduce the heat then add the red chillies until they change colour and then the green chilli, stirring for a few seconds.

Add the reserved first smooth masala paste and stir well for a few minutes.

The paste will bubble and splutter, so do keep a lid handy. Continue to sauté the paste, scraping the base and sides well with a flat wooden or plastic spatula until you see oil being released at the sides. This shows that the paste is cooked.

Now add the 500 ml (17 fl oz/2¼ cups) water, stir well and taste the sauce.

Bring the sauce to a slow boil and immerse the previously sautéed chicken pieces and the halved cherry tomatoes, cover and cook over a gentle heat until chicken is cooked through and tender, about 30 minutes. If necessary, lift out the chicken and boil the sauce rapidly for a few minutes until reduced and thickened. Taste and re-season, if necessary.

Meanwhile, par-boil the potatoes for about 5 minutes until nearly tender, then drain and dry well on paper towels. Heat oil for deep-frying and fry the potatoes for about 6 minutes or until crisp and golden. Drain on paper towels and toss with a little salt.

Serve the chicken with the fried potatoes and some bread or chapattis on its own or with other dishes.

CHAANP NA CUTLESS

LAMB CUTLETS WITH POTATOES

Serves 4

Parsee-style lamb cutlets! Succulent little chops, covered with spiced mashed potato, rolled in semolina, fried and served with onion and tomato gravy. If you only have coarse semolina, whiz it in a food processor or clean coffee grinder to refine. Breadcrumbs can also be used.

Peel and slice the potatoes and boil until really tender (up to 10 minutes depending on thickness). Drain and return to the same pan over a medium heat.

Stir continuously, scraping from the bottom with a wooden spatula until the potatoes are totally dry. Now mash or pass through a ricer and set aside in a wide dish to cool. Refrigerate when at room temperature but do not cover (if you place them in a small bowl the sides will sweat and make your mash wet again).

Blend the ground spices with a little salt and the ginger and garlic paste and rub all over the cutlets. Leave in a covered container in the refrigerator for at least 2 hours or overnight.

Split 2 of the green chillies in quarters lengthways. Heat about 1½ tablespoons oil in a large frying pan over a medium heat and, when hot, add the cinnamon and the split chillies. When the cinnamon darkens and the chillies change colour scrape all excess marinade off the lamb cutlets and brown the meat on both sides, taking care not to keep the oil too hot as this will cause the marinade to burn. Take care not to agitate the pan too much either. By doing so the pan will cool down and the chops will begin to stew rather than sauté.

When the chops are coloured and sealed remove them and add the onions to the pan along with the marinade that was scraped off the chops. Add a little water to deglaze the pan, Stir and scrape up any sediment. The water will evaporate as the onions sauté.

When the onion is soft, about 5 minutes, add the chopped tomatoes and cook until both the onion and the tomato are thoroughly cooked. Add a bit more water from time to time so as to get a sauce of pouring consistency. Check seasoning and discard the cinnamon sticks and the green chillies. Set aside and reheat just before serving.

Stir half the chopped coriander into the mashed potatoes, the rest into the sauce.

Mince or finely chop the remaining green chilli with the toasted cumin seeds and mix into the mashed potato. Season to taste.

Now divide the potato into the same number of portions as there are chops. Press a portion of potato around the meat end only of the cutlets, leaving the bone ends free. Coat each chop in flour, then in beaten egg and then into the semolina.

Heat about 2.5 cm (1 in) oil in a large, deep frying pan and fry the chops until golden and crisp, about 6 minutes, turning once. Serve with some salad if you like and the tomato and onion gravy.

4–5 large, fairly floury
all-purpose potatoes

½ tsp ground turmeric

1 heaped tsp ground cumin

2 heaped tsp ground coriander

1 heaped tsp chilli powder

salt to taste

2 tbsp ginger and garlic paste
(see page 157)
(or 6 garlic cloves, crushed and 1 tbsp
grated fresh ginger)

8–12 French trimmed lamb cutlets

3 long, thin green chillies

vegetable or rapeseed oil for frying

2 x 5 cm (2 in) pieces cinnamon
stick, as desired

1 onion, very finely chopped

2 tbsp chopped coriander
(cilantro leaves)

4–5 tomatoes, finely chopped

1 level tsp cumin seeds, lightly toasted

100–150 g (3½–5 oz/1–1½ cups)
plain (all-purpose) flour

3–4 eggs, beaten

100–150 g (3½–5 oz/scant–generous
1 cup) fine semolina or breadcrumbs

To serve

salad, sliced tomato and onion gravy

AUNTY DOLLY'S EAST INDIAN CURRY

MUDH ISLAND KOAMBDI CURRY

Serves 4–6

Aunty Dolly or Dolly Aunty as we called her, was the wife of Dad's good friend and second-in-command of the Western India Automobile Association. They were very dear friends and I spent many-a-day in their house. She made amazing food and I remember her best dish being her super-fabulous coconut pancakes.

Mudh Island, also known as Honey Island, is along the coast just north of Bombay. The community is mostly Koli or Fisherfolk and Roman Catholic. Converted to Christianity by the Portuguese in the 16th and 17th centuries, the Roman Catholics still have certain customary masalas and spice blends, which also make their cuisine unique. To this day in the metropolis of Mumbai, there exists a tiny village called Matharpacadi within this huge city that has remained untouched for centuries. Though I have not tried it, I believe that there is a traditional East Indian restaurant there too.

You can make double the quantity of this masala and store for several weeks in the refrigerator in a sterilized screw-topped jar with a layer of sunflower or olive oil over to preserve it.

First make the masala. Heat oil in a large frying pan or wok until a haze forms. Add the onion and sauté over a medium heat until soft but not brown, about 4 minutes. Reduce the heat. Add the garlic and sauté until just turning golden. Remove from the heat. Leave to cool then tip into a blender or small food processor with all the remaining masala ingredients. Grind to a smooth, thick paste, adding a little water as necessary (but not too much as it must not be runny). Set aside.

To make the curry, if using chicken, no need to marinate first. If using beef or lamb, rub the meat all over with the masala, cover and leave in the refrigerator to marinate for several hours or overnight.

Heat the oil in a heavy-based saucepan or flameproof casserole. Add the onion and sauté until soft and lightly golden, about 5 minutes. If using chicken, stir the masala into the pan and sauté for several minutes until the oil runs again.

Add 150 ml (5 fl oz/⅔ cup) water and the coconut milk and bring to the boil. Add the chicken, pushing it down well into the sauce, part-cover and simmer for 30–40 minutes or until the chicken is tender and cooked through. Taste and re-season if necessary.

If using the marinated meat, add to the browned onions and sauté until browned all over and the juices have dried up, scraping the pan well with a wooden spatula to prevent sticking and burning. Add enough water to three-quarters cover the meat, bring to the boil, reduce the heat to low, part-cover and simmer very gently for about 45 minutes until almost tender. Stir in the coconut milk, bring back to the boil, reduce the heat and continue to simmer for a further 30 minutes or until the meat is really tender and bathed in a rich sauce. Add a splash more water if drying out. Taste and re-season as necessary.

Sprinkle the chicken or meat curry with the chopped coriander and serve with steamed rice.

For the masala
2 tbsp sunflower or rapeseed oil
1 onion, thinly sliced
1 large garlic clove, chopped
1½ tbsp coriander seeds
¼ tsp cumin seeds
generous pinch of fennel seeds
generous pinch of ground turmeric
2 cloves
pinch of fenugreek seeds
generous pinch of black mustard seeds
5–6 black peppercorns
½ small red pepper or 1 dried red chilli,
roughly chopped

For the curry
2–3 tbsp sunflower or rapeseed oil
2 onions, thinly sliced
4–5 chicken portions, skin removed,
if preferred, or 600 g (1 lb 5 oz)
lean diced lamb or beef
400 ml can of coconut milk
2 tbsp chopped coriander
(cilantro) leaves

To serve
Boiled Rice (see page 195)

DHAANSAAK

RICE WITH LENTILS AND LAMB

Serves 4–6

The best known recipe of great Parsee cooking –
it's the traditional Sunday roast. *Dhaansaak* is made
up of two main parts: lamb with lentils and rice.
Each one can be used as an independent dish as
well so I have kept each part separate. This will
not only simplify things but make you understand
the depth and intricacies of Indian cooking.
Both masalas in the recipes can be prepared in
larger quantities and kept for the future in sealed
containers: the paste in the refrigerator, the dry mix
in a dark storecupboard. The browned rice is good
with other meat and poultry dishes too.

To a Parsee, *Dhaansaak* is always made with lamb
unless someone in the family does not eat lamb, or
is a vegetarian. The accompaniments – the little
lamb kebab balls and the kachumber (onion salad)
are as important as the main part – a bit like having
Yorkshire puddings and horseradish sauce with roast
beef! Cooking *Dhaansaak* is a painstaking affair
but very straightforward if you follow each section
methodically and it can be started the day before to
enjoy the Sunday lunch (which is what we Parsees
do). The end result can be a sheer achievement and
if done well with go down as a masterpiece.

Top right: Brown Onion Pulao (page 92)

Centre: Spiced Lentils Cooked with Spicy Lamb (page 90)

Bottom left: Kachumber (page 93)

Bottom right: Kebeb Balls (page 93)

MASALA NI DAAR SAATHAY GOS

SPICED LENTILS COOKED WITH SPICY LAMB

PART 1: THE 'SAAK'

For the masala

5 cm (2 in) piece of cinnamon stick

6 green cardamom pods, split 6–8 cloves

2 tsp cumin seeds

10 black peppercorns

1 heaped tbsp coriander seeds

8–10 large red chillies

7.5 cm (3 in) piece of fresh ginger, roughly chopped

10–12 garlic cloves, roughly chopped

30–50 g (1–2 oz) bunch of coriander (cilantro)

Serves 4–6

First prepare the masala. Toast all the ingredients except the fresh coriander in a dry frying pan or wok, stirring for a few minutes until fragrant and lightly browned but not burnt. Cool slightly then tip into a clean coffee grinder or small food processor and grind to a paste, adding a little water and stopping and scraping down the sides as necessary. Alternatively, pound the mixture in a mortar with a pestle or in a small bowl with the end of a rolling pin. Do not add too much water or it will become runny. Set aside.

Next make the daal. Wash all the lentils and transfer to a large flameproof casserole. Add water to come 2.5 cm (1 in) above the level of the lentils. Add all the remaining ingredients and bring to the boil. Reduce the heat and simmer until tender, about 30 minutes.

Whilst cooking, scrape the bottom occasionally with a wooden spatula to prevent sticking. When the lentils are fully soft, purée with a hand blender and set aside.

Meanwhile, cook the lamb. Heat the oil in a heavy-based saucepan and fry the lamb on all sides to brown. When the meat is sealed, add the prepared masala paste. Sauté until you see the oil run (this shows the masala is cooked).

Add the water and a little salt. Bring to the boil, reduce the heat to medium, cover and cook gently for 20–25 minutes or until tender, adding a little more water as necessary and stirring occasionally until bathed in a rich sauce.

Blend the lamb with the daal. This is your *saak*. Set aside and reheat when ready to serve (you may need to add a little more water, if necessary) then transfer to a hot serving dish. This is also good on its own with rice as a main course.

For the daal

100 g (3½ oz/⅔ cup) yellow lentils
(toor daal)
50 g (2 oz/¼ cup) split chickpeas
(garbanzos) or yellow split peas
(channa daal)
50 g(2 oz/¼ cup) split yellow mung
beans (moong daal)
100 g (3½ oz/scant ½ cup) red lentils
(masoor daal)
1 small aubergine (eggplant), diced
100 g (3½ oz/⅔ cup) red kuri, diced
(or other winter squash)
2 tbsp coarsely chopped dill (dillweed)
1 taro leaf (optional)
50 g (2 oz) fresh fenugreek (methi)
leaves, or 1 tbsp dried
salt to taste
1 tbsp tamarind paste
100g (3½ oz/scant ½ cup jaggery
or muscovado sugar
2 tbsp chopped coriander (cilantro)
leaves and stalks
2 tbsp chopped mint leaves

For the lamb

2–3 tbsp sunflower or rapeseed oil
500 g (1lb 2 oz) lean lamb (preferably
leg) cut in 2 cm (¾ in) pieces
150 ml (5 fl/⅔ cup) water
salt to taste

VAGHARAELA CHAAWAL

BROWN ONION PULAO

PART 2: THE 'DHAAN' AND PIECING TOGETHER OF YOUR DHAANSAAK

Serves 4–6

Heat the oil in a flameproof casserole and add the spices. Sauté for a minute or two over a medium heat until browned and fragrant. Add the onions and sauté gently until they are a deep brown, about 10 minutes.

Add the rice and sauté for 5–6 minutes, turning regularly so that all the grains get evenly cooked and coated in the oil and onions.

Add hot water up to 2.5 cm (1 in) above the level of the rice, season with salt, stir well, bring back to the boil, reduce the heat to low, cover and cook gently for 15–20 minutes. Check occasionally, stirring gently from the bottom up with a flat wooden spatula and slowly add a little more water if necessary. Remove from the heat and set aside in the covered pot. I find that a more effective technique is to put the covered pot in middle shelf of a pre-heated oven. Cook for 20 minutes at a 130°C/266°F/gas ½ heat and then switch off. If in doubt, use double the amount of water that there is to rice.

Meanwhile, make the masala (this can be done in advance if preferred). Toast all the spices in a dry frying pan, stirring for a minute or two until fragrant. Cool then tip into a clean coffee grinder or small food processor (or use a mortar with a pestle or small bowl with the end of a rolling pin) and grind to a powder. Set aside.

When nearly ready to serve, separate the sliced onions into rings. Heat the oil in a frying pan until hazy and sauté the onions over a high heat until crisp and golden. Drain on paper towels.

Sprinkle the garam masala over the rested pulao and stir through gently. Garnish with the browned onions and chopped herbs and serve. This is your *dhaan*. It is also good served with any other daal or curry or, even, with just cooked chicken or prawns stirred through and heated thoroughly.

For the pulao

75 ml (2 fl oz/⅓ cup) sunflower or rapeseed oil

2.5 cm (1 in) piece of cinnamon stick

3–4 green cardamom pods, split

3–4 cloves

4–5 star anise

2 onions, halved and thinly sliced

500 g (1lb 2 oz/2¼ cups) basmati rice, washed and drained

2 tsp salt or to taste

For the garam masala

3–4 green cardamom pods, split and seeds extracted

3–4 cloves

2–3 star anise

1 heaped tsp cumin seeds

8–10 black peppercorns

2–3 dried red chillies

2 tsp dried fenugreek (methi) leaves

For the garnish

1–2 onions, sliced

2 tbsp sunflower or rapeseed oil

2 tbsp chopped coriander (cilantro) leaves

2 tbsp chopped mint leaves

TO FINSIH THE DHAANSAAK

Make the kebab mixture as in the original recipe but shape into 2.5 cm (1 in) balls. Either deep-fry in hot oil for 3–4 minutes or until golden and cooked through.

Drain on paper towels or put on a baking tray and bake in a preheated oven at 200°C/400°F/gas 6 for about 20 minutes. Arrange on top of the pulao or put in a separate dish and garnish with coriander leaves.

For the kachamber put all the ingredients in a serving bowl and toss together well. Taste and adjust vinegar and salt if necessary.

To serve the *Dhaansaak*, assemble all the dishes on the table with the family seated around, and allow everyone to help themselves. You may also like to serve some crisp lentil papadums (not the Madras type) and some fruity chutney along side the meal.

For the kebab balls
1 quantity Seekh Kevâab mixture
(see page 173)
a few coriander (cilantro)
leaves (optional)

For the kachumber
1 large onion, halved and thinly sliced
2 tbsp chopped coriander (cilantro) leaves
2 tbsp chopped mint leaves
1 green chilli, seeded if liked,
and finely chopped
1 small tomato, seeded and finely chopped
1 tsp vinegar (just a splash)
salt to taste

2 tsp ground cumin

2 tsp ground coriander

250 ml (8½ fl oz/1 cup) warm water

1 tsp cumin seeds

2–3 large floury potatoes

100 ml (3½ fl oz/scant ½ cup)
    double (heavy) cream

3–4 egg yolks

salt to taste

2 tbsp sunflower or rapeseed oil

2 x 5 cm (2 in) pieces of cinnamon stick

2–3 whole dried red chillies,
    broken into pieces and seeded

2 red onions, finely chopped

10 cm (4 in) piece of fresh ginger,
    finely chopped

2 garlic cloves, finely chopped

500 g (1 lb 2 oz) lean minced
    (ground) lamb

2 tomatoes, chopped

8–10 sprigs of chopped coriander
    (cilantro)

GINGER COUNTRY CAPTAIN

GINGER COTTAGE PIE

Serves 4

This is an Anglo-Indian dish with no real Indian equivalent name. It will make you see the British favourite in a completely different light and, again, allow you see how diverse and inclusive Indian cooking can be.

Blend the ground cumin and coriander with the water in a small jug and set aside. Toast the cumin seeds gently in a dry frying pan for about 30 seconds until fragrant. Cool then crush in a mortar with a pestle (or in a small bowl with the end of a rolling pin). Set aside.

Boil the potatoes in plenty of water until the skins crack, drain well, peel whilst still hot by holding in paper towels or a clean cloth then pass through a potato ricer into a bowl or mash thoroughly with a potato masher.

Whisk the cream and egg yolks together thoroughly and then beat into the potato until smooth and lump free. Add the crushed cumin and season to taste.

Heat the oil in a flameproof casserole. When a haze forms add the cinnamon and sauté for a minute until it changes colour but does not blacken or burn, turn heat down to medium and add the red chilli pieces. Stir for a few seconds then add the onion. Sauté until the onion is soft and pale, 4–5 minutes, then add the ginger and garlic and sauté for 2–3 minutes until both are pale golden brown.

Reduce the heat to low and add the mince and prepared spice water. Break the mince up as much as you can so that you see no lumps and turn the heat up to medium, but continue stirring and breaking up until all the meat is separate.

Bring to the boil, reduce the heat to medium and simmer, stirring every now and again so no lumps form, until the mixture is nearly dry. Stir in the chopped tomatoes and simmer for a few minutes until the tomato is pulpy. Season to taste and add the chopped coriander. Transfer to a flameproof serving dish.

Preheat the grill (broiler). Spread out the meat evenly in the dish, then either spread the creamed potato on top and rough up with a fork or pipe it. Cook under the grill until golden brown, about 5 minutes. Alternatively, preheat the oven to 190°C/375°F/gas 5 and bake for about 35 minutes. Rotate the dish to get an even colouring.

For the lentils and lamb

300–350 g (1½ –1¾ cups) whole red
lentils or puy lentils

1 kg (2 lb 3 oz) diced leg of lamb

2 heaped tbsp ginger and garlic paste
(see page 157) or use 6–8 garlic
cloves, crushed and 1 heaped tbsp
grated fresh ginger

1 tsp salt

2 tbsp sunflower or rapeseed oil

hot water, or lamb or chicken stock

For the masala

2 tbsp sunflower or rapeseed oil

7.5–10 cm (3–4 in) piece of
cinnamon stick

3–4 green cardamom pods,
split or lightly crushed

3–4 cloves, roughly crushed

2–3 dried long red chillies

2–3 green chillies, split in
half lengthways

3 onions, finely chopped

2 tbsp water

2 tsp ground cumin

1 tbsp ground coriander

¾ tsp ground turmeric

1 heaped tsp chilli powder

1–2 tsp caster (superfine) sugar

2–3 tomatoes, chopped (optional)

salt to taste

2 heaped tbsp chopped
coriander (cilantro) leaves

large knob of butter

To serve

chapattis (see pages 183 or 185) or
Boiled Rice (see page 195)

MASOOR MA GOS

LAMB COOKED WITH INDIAN PUY LENTILS

Serves 6

Masoor is the whole lentil which is pink when skinned. Often called Pigeon Pea, it is a smaller cousin of puy lentils so glamorized by French cuisine. Indian cooking uses lentils and pulses a great deal and no one does more so than the Parsee community. Cooked with lamb here, the lentils can also be cooked with sheep's tongue or chicken, or just cooked plain with some potatoes as a vegetarian option. This brings back memories of our family dining as a child. Our dad loved Masoor so we had them often. Plus it was cheap and very filling!

Wash and soak the lentils in tepid water to come about 1 cm (½ in) above the level of the lentils for an hour or two, if you have time (it is not vital but I prefer them this way).

Clean wash and drain the lamb well. Rub it all over with the ginger and garlic paste and salt and set aside to marinate.

After about an hour heat the oil in a flameproof casserole until nearly smoking and add the lamb, sauté well but remember that the ginger and garlic paste will stick so keep deglazing with a little water, scraping up the sediment from the base of the pan, and continue sautéing until browned. Add enough water or stock to almost cover the meat, bring to the boil, reduce the heat and simmer gently until the lamb is almost tender, about 30 minutes. Transfer to a bowl and clean the casserole for the next stage.

Prepare the masala. Heat the oil in the casserole and when a haze forms, add the cinnamon, cardamom and cloves and sauté for about 30 seconds until fragrant then add the red and green chillies and continue to fry until the red chilli changes colour. Add the onions and the water and sauté until onions are soft pale or light brown.

Blend the ground cumin, coriander, turmeric and chilli powder in a few table-spoons of water to form a smooth thin paste and add this to the sautéing onions. Continue to cook until tiny bubbles of the oil are released and the aroma changes from smelling the raw powders to a deep cooked aroma.

Add the soaked lentils and their soaking water and mix in well. Add a little more water, if needed, but they should, ideally, cook just as they are. Bring to the boil, reduce the heat and simmer until tender, about 20 minutes.

Once the lentils are cooked add the cooked lamb and check the seasoning. Add the chopped tomato if using, the chopped coriander and a good knob of butter. Stir well and season to suit. Serve with chapattis or rice.

ASSADO DE PORCO

ROAST LOIN OF PORK GOAN STYLE

Serves 6–8

There is many a recipe secret used by Goan mamas to make a signature dish, yet they are still based on the original Portuguese version introduced during their occupation. The Goans' love for pork also stems back to the time of the Portuguese settlers. Whilst *Assado de Porco* generally refers to the loin, one can use rolled shoulder or, even, lean belly. If using belly, you will need two bellies as they are smaller, in which case, marinate individually and proceed as normal (it may need the longer cooking time to become tender). I do strongly recommend belly pork as it is fabulous and tast yet highly underrated.

Break the cinnamon into small pieces. Add to a mortar along with the peppercorns and cloves and crush coarsely with a pestle (or use a small bowl with the end of a rolling pin). Gently toast this mixture in a dry frying pan over a low heat and add the red chillies. Toast, stirring, until fragrant and changing colour. Remove from the heat and tip into a small dish to cool.

In a blender or small food processor, add the ginger, garlic, onion, green chillies, turmeric and the cooled spice blend, tamarind pulp, vinegar, half the oil, the sugar and salt and purée to a relatively fine paste.

Unroll the pork and rub plenty of the masala well into the flesh and set it aside in the refrigerator to marinate for a few hours, if you have the time. Roll up and tie again.

Mix the remaining masala with the potatoes (and pumpkin and onions, if using). Preheat the oven to 180°C/350°F/gas 4. Place a large roasting tin onto the top of the cooker, add the remaining oil and tilt to coat the tin.

Scrape the excess masala off the marinated pork into the marinated potatoes and brown the pork well on all sides.

Keeping the pork in the centre of the tray spread the marinated potatoes all around and place in the oven. Roast for about 1½–2 hours until tender.

When the pork is cooked remove separately and check the potatoes. Taste (they might need some seasoning), and add the fresh chopped coriander.

Serve the pork sliced surrounded with the potatoes.

For the masala

10 cm (4 in) piece of cinnamon stick

1 heaped tsp black peppercorns

5–6 cloves

4–5 large dried chillies,
broken in pieces

10 cm (4 in) piece of fresh ginger

6–8 garlic cloves

3–4 small red onions, roughly chopped

2 longish green chillies

1 heaped tsp ground turmeric

100 ml (3½ fl oz/scant ½ cup) fresh
tamarind pulp (see page 59)

200 ml (7 fl oz/scant 1 cup) palm or
cider (apple cider) vinegar

100 ml (3½ fl oz/scant ½ cup)

2 tbsp sunflower or rapeseed oil

1 tbsp muscovado sugar

1 tbsp salt

2 kg (4½ lb) pork loin, shoulder or belly,
rind removed, boned and rolled

8 waxy potatoes, peeled and
cut into chunks

300–400 g (10½ –14 oz) pumpkin,
seeded, peeled, if liked,
and cut into chunks (optional)

3–4 small red onions, peeled
and quartered (optional)

3 tbsp chopped coriander
(cilantro) leaves

1–1.25 kg (2 lb 3 oz–2 lb 8 oz)
   knuckle-end half leg of lamb

1 tsp cumin seeds

1 tbsp coriander seeds

6–8 large red chillies, cut into pieces

50 g (2 oz) fresh ginger,
   roughly chopped

50 g (2 oz) garlic cloves

12 or more small potatoes

2–3 tbsp sunflower or rapeseed oil

2 x 2.5 cm (1 in) pieces of cinnamon stick

3–4 green cardamom pods, split

2–3 cloves

3–4 black peppercorns

water, or lamb or chicken stock,
   as necessary

3 onions, chopped

200 g (7 oz) tomatoes, chopped
   (or a small can)

1 tsp salt

2 tbsp coriander (cilantro)
   leaves, chopped

To serve

Boiled Rice (page 195)

MASALA NU ROAST GOS

SLOW-COOKED SHANK OF LAMB MASALA

Serves 6–8

This is a Parsee-style roasted joint of lamb. Once roasted, the lamb may be sliced and served cold as a sandwich filler or served hot with the gravy and potatoes shown opposite and boiled rice. This style of marinating is quite typical but very adaptable and the simplicity of it all makes it suitable for most meats or a whole chicken.

Trim the leg of lamb of fat, if necessary.

Toast the cumin, coriander seeds and red chilli in a dry frying pan over a low heat for about 30 seconds until fragrant and just changing colour. Tip out of the pam and cool.

In a clean coffee grinder or small food processor, grind together the ginger, garlic and the roasted cumin, coriander and chilli to a fine paste with only a splash of water to form a thick paste. Set aside.

Peel the potatoes, remove any spots, wash and keep them covered in cold water. In a large, flameproof casserole big enough to take the leg of lamb add the oil and heat until a light haze forms. Reduce the heat a little and add the leg of lamb. Brown well on all sides until the meat is well sealed and coloured.

Remove the lamb from the casserole and add the whole spices. Sauté for a minute or so over a low heat until the cloves swell slightly, then deglaze the casserole with a little water, lamb or chicken stock, and scrape up any sediment from the base of the pan with a wooden spatula.

Add the onions and continue to cook until the liquid evaporates and the onions are now being sautéed. When soft, about 5 minutes, add the masala paste and salt. Deglaze the container with a little water and tip it into the casserole too. Continue cooking for about 5 minutes, stirring, until the oil is released again.

Preheat the oven to 180°C/350°F/gas 4. Cook the lamb in the oven for 15 minutes then remove and turn the meat over, adding a little water or stock, if necessary, to prevent it drying out. Coat it well with the masala. Cook for a further 30 minutes. The lamb should be approximately half cooked.

Add the chopped tomatoes and the potatoes and, if necessary, a little more water or stock. Cover and continue cooking for a further 10–15 minutes. Check if the meat is cooked. If not using a thermometer the best way to test the lamb is to check the shrinkage and texture. When the lamb is almost cooked the muscles at the shin will have retracted from the bone and the lamb will feel soft to the touch. If in doubt, insert a thin skewer or a roasting fork and check to see if the fluid released is running clear (pink lamb is OK). When the lamb is done transfer it to a carving dish and remove any gravy stuck to it. Remove the potatoes and keep warm.

Spoon off any fat from the gravy. Check the consistency and, if necessary, add enough water or stock to give a pouring consistency. Boil it over a high heat for a minute or two and add little freshly chopped coriander for a touch of magic.

40 g (1½ oz/3 tbsp) butter

2 tsp chilli powder

1 tsp caster (superfine) sugar

½ tsp salt

200 g (7 oz/scant 1 cup) tomato purée

juice of ½ lime

5–7.5 cm (2–3 in) piece of fresh ginger,
    grated or finely chopped

1 heaped tsp cumin seeds, toasted
    and ground

2–3 green chillies, finely chopped (plus 1–2
    extra split and added for flavour, optional)

200 ml (7 fl oz/scant 1 cup) double
    (heavy) cream

Chicken Tikka (see page 25)

1 heaped tbsp chopped coriander (cilantro)

BUTTER CHICKEN

BUTTER CHICKEN MASALA

Serves 4

The classic Butter Chicken from North India, Chicken Makhani, is a bit different as well as a bit more subtle than this. The Butter Chicken Masala of Bombay is so well known it does not even have any other Indian term for it. Ideally use the cooked Chickeny Tikka recipe in this book (see page 25) but you could instead marinate 4 cubed chicken breasts in 4 heaped tablespoons of thick plain yoghurt with 1 tablespoon of tandoori paste and then grill it like the tikka. Butter Chicken in Bombay was made famous by the one and only Delhi Durbar restaurant. Please do not think of calories when cooking this dish as the word does not exist here!

Heat the butter in a kadai, wok or large deep frying pan until it foams.

Remove from the heat and add the chilli powder, sugar and salt, stir well and put back onto the heat, stirring and cooking for a minute or so, then add the tomato purée and lime juice and cook for 2 minutes over a low heat, stirring well.

Add the ginger, half the cumin and the chopped chillies and cook over a low heat until the butter separates slightly. Add the split chillies, if using, and the cream and simmer for 6–8 minutes. Discard the split chillies.

Add the cooked chicken tikka meat, and heat through until piping hot. Taste and re-season, if necessary. Sprinkle with the chopped coriander and the remaining toasted ground cumin.

MURGHI NA FARCHA

PARSEE FRIED CHICKEN

Serves 4

This is the classical Parsee-style fried chicken much loved by all at most festive or celebratory occasions. When served with the traditional tomato sauce (see page 29), it could well be an Italian speciality. It's a dish that showcases our old Persian roots and, again, shows how wonderful Indian cooking can be. Serve as a starter or as part of a selection of dishes for a main course.

Grind all the masala ingredients in a clean coffee grinder or small food processor, or in a mortar with a pestle (or in a small bowl with the end of a rolling pin), adding a little water to form a thick paste (don't add too much or the result will be runny). Set aside.

Remove the skin from the chicken, if you like and cut the meat into thin strips or into pieces or halves. Rub the masala paste into the chicken and leave to marinate in the refrigerator for at least 30 minutes or up to 6 hours. (Bigger pieces will need more time to marinate.)

Heat the oil for deep-frying in a kadai, wok or large, deep frying pan (if large enough you can cook the chicken in one go, if not fry in batches and remove any floating bits of egg and blackened residues between batches, and reheat the oil slowly so it doesn't foam up).

Beat two eggs at a time for best results. This gives a crispier and more frilly coating. Test the oil by dropping a little egg into it – the egg should rise and sizzle instantly.

Dip each piece of chicken into flour and then into the beaten egg and fry in hot oil. Try one piece first and see if the temperature is correct. Very hot oil will discolour too fast and not cook the meat. If the pieces are large then care needs to be taken. Put large pieces in an oven and heat at 120°C/248°F/ ½ until then meat is thoroughly cooked.

After adding the chicken, lower the heat slightly and keep spooning the hot oil over the chicken to get frilled edges. Cook until crisp and golden, about 3 minutes.

Remove with a slotted spoon and drain on paper towels.

Serve with a wedges of lime and some tomato sauce, and/or some salad with a mayonnaise-based dressing.

For the masala

100 g (3½ oz) fresh ginger, chopped

6 garlic cloves

3–4 thin hot green chillies, seeded

1½ tbsp ground turmeric

4 tsp cumin seeds, toasted

few sprigs of coriander (cilantro) or
a small pile of the stalks only

juice of ½ lime

salt to taste

4 chicken leg portions, boned and
halved at the joint, or
8 boned thighs

4 eggs

plain (all-purpose) flour, as required

vegetable oil for deep-frying

To serve

wedges of lime and tomato sauce
(see page 29), and/or salad with a
mayonnaise-based dressing

VEGETABLES

'Vegetarianism' is a term ideally suited or even coined for India! Whilst we are all not vegetarians perhaps it might be safe to say that India has about five to six hundred million vegetarians, though I do believe it is much more.

My ultimate aim is to one day have the privilege of time and money to drive around India, exploring all the different types of food that locals eat. The knowledge and learning would be mind-blowing.

Bombay, a massive melting pot of a city, perhaps consumes the maximum amount of meat and poultry in the nation: but vegetables are also everywhere, in the form of snacks, light meals, Thalis, roadside creations, the veritable Bombay sandwich (page 158) and so on. Even a devout meat-eater can be seen wolfing down tasty vegetarian delicacies, unable to resist the vast array of food at their disposable. With the many communities that reside in Bombay, there are hundreds and thousands of meals all sold in this magnificent city, so you really are spoilt for choice.

The local or indigenous population – the Maharashtrians – have an amazing range of traditional vegetarian dishes. Whilst I am also a Maharashtrian Parsee per say, I am ashamed to say that I know very little about their cuisine except perhaps a few more common dishes.

No matter where you happen to live, you will no doubt have access to some fabulous vegetables throughout the year. Seasonality is the secret, and this is something Indian women pride themselves on as they create wonderful dishes with in-season vegetables and refuse to touch them when they are not.

I urge you to scour the markets and the stores where you shop and try out a multitude of different types. You will be astounded at just how much variety there is available to you and I can guarentee that you will definitely notice the difference. For instance, when you buy asparagus that's in season, as opposed to lesser varieties that travel hundreds of thousands of miles to supermarkets. Brussels sprouts are so good when treated differently instead of boiling them to death. Shred them with a few cumin seeds and green chilli, which will give them a fabulous lift, and cook for no longer than four to five minutes.

Buy fresh wholesome produce and enjoy the flavours that only seasonality can bring and avoid stored, semi-ripe produce exported from way across the globe, unless absolutely necessary. We do serve seasonal vegetables in the restaurants and find this to be a very soul-satisfying exercise, of making use of the best of Nature's bounty when it is supposed to be eaten.

2 tbsp sesame seeds

750 g (1 lb 10 oz) Pink Fir Apple potatoes

3 tbsp sunflower or rapeseed oil

1 tsp cumin seeds

2–3 green chillies, split in quarters,
   lengthways

7.5 cm (3 in) piece of fresh ginger, grated

15–20 curry leaves (preferably fresh),
   shredded

¼ tsp ground asafoetida

3 onions, thinly sliced

salt to taste

2 plum tomatoes, chopped (optional)

1 tbsp chopped coriander (cilantro) leaves

ALOO TIL TINKA

PINK FIR APPLE POTATO WITH TOASTED SESAME SEEDS

Serves 4

This recipe is designed to bring out the best in the Pink Fir Apple, which is the king amongst fingerling potatoes. Slender and thin it delivers a fabulous texture and taste if handled delicately and not too heavily spiced. You can, of course, use other similar varieties with very good results!

Place the sesame seeds in a baking tray and toast in the oven at 140°C /275°F/ gas 1 for 10 minutes, then switch off the oven, leaving the tray inside for a further 10 minutes but making sure the seeds don't burn and you stir them about regularly. Alternatively, toast in a dry frying pan over a medium heat, stirring until just golden then tip out of the pan immediately to prevent burning.

Cut the potatoes into small dice.

Heat the oil in a large pan. When a haze forms but it is not smoking, add the cumin seeds and stir briefly then add the chilli, ginger, curry leaves and asafoetida. Stir for a few seconds until the crackling stops then add the onions and sauté for about 3 minutes until lightly golden and then add in the potatoes.

Continue to sauté until the potatoes are evenly coated in the mixture. Season with salt and add enough water to half-cover the potatoes (do not add too much, as you want a nicely moist but not wet potato after cooking). Bring to the boil, cover tightly with a lid, reduce the heat and simmer for about 10 minutes until nearly cooked. Gently stir from time to time to rotate the potatoes so as to avoid uneven cooking.

Remove the lid, add the chopped tomatoes, if using, and continue to cook in the open pan until the potatoes are tender and bathed in just a little thickened liquid. Add the toasted sesame seeds and mix well. Check the seasoning and stir in the fresh coriander. Serve hot.

CHOTTA ALOO RASSA

BABY POTATOES IN A TANGY TOMATO SAUCE

Serves 2 as a main couse / 4 as an accompaniment

In every vegetable market, you will find that the baby potatoes and onions have been seperated out. They will not always be fully-ripe, but they do make an excellent dish when cooked in a tomato-based sauce. This is a simple recipe and can be made with any variety of baby potatoes. However, Jersey Royal varieties do not work with this recipe.

Peel and parboil the potatoes in just enough water to cover them for about 8 minutes. Lift out the part-cooked potatoes with a slotted spoon and set aside. Boil the water rapidly until well reduced and soupy. Set aside.

Heat the oil in a saucepan until it forms a haze, add the mustard seeds and when they crackle add the curry leaves, the cumin and lovage seeds. Stir briefly then add the chillies, garlic and ginger.

As the garlic begins to colour, add the onion and sauté until soft and golden. Add the tomato juice, the potato liquor and the chopped tomatoes. Simmer until pulpy.

Add the part-cooked potatoes and salt to taste, and simmer for about 10 minutes until tender. Taste and re-season if necessary.

Sprinkle over the mint and coriander and remove from the heat but keep the pot covered unless it is being served immediately.

200 g (7 oz) baby potatoes, peeled
2 tbsp sunflower oil
½ tsp black mustard seeds
6–8 curry leaves, preferably fresh
1 tsp cumin seeds
1 tsp ajwain or lovage (carom) seeds
2 green chillies, split and seeded
6 garlic cloves, chopped
20 g (¾ oz) fresh ginger, chopped
1 onion, chopped
250 ml (8½ fl oz/1 cup) tomato juice
1–2 tomatoes, chopped
2 tsp mint leaves, chopped
1 tbsp chopped coriander
(cilantro) leaves
salt to taste

FOOGATH

CABBAGE & BEAN WITH FRESH COCONUT

Serves 4–6

Foogath just means any vegetable dish cooked with curry leaves and coconut. The Portuguese word *refogado* stood for something cooked in oil, and I believe *Foogath* stemmed from this. It is often made just with cabbage or beans but I love the combination of both as a delicious side dish.

It is also delicious as a light snack meal with hot crusty rolls.

If using desiccated coconut, soak in 150 ml (5 fl oz/²⁄₃ cup) water for 1 hour until soft and rehydrated and the water is absorbed.

Shred the cabbage after removing the core and any thick stalks. Top and tail the beans and cut in 2.5 cm (1 in) pieces. Do not mix the two vegetables. Heat the oil in a casserole or heavy-based saucepan and, when hazy, add the mustard seeds. After they stop crackling, reduce the heat to medium, add the curry leaves, the cumin and the red chilli pieces.

Sauté for a minute and add the sliced onions and sauté until soft but not brown, about 3 minutes. Add the garlic and sauté for a minute or two then add the turmeric and the cabbage.

Sauté the cabbage for a minute or two and then add the coconut. Sauté for 4–5 minutes, by this time the cabbage will be more than half done, then mix in the French beans and check the seasoning. Cook for a further 2 minutes or until the beans are just tender but still have some 'bite' and remain bright green.

Sprinkle with a few drops of lime juice and add the coriander. Cover the pan, remove from the heat and leave covered for 4–5 minutes to allow the flavours to develop.

⅔ coconut, freshly grated or 150 g
(5 oz/1⅔ cups) desiccated
(shredded) coconut

250–300 g cabbage

250 g (9 oz) French beans

2 tbsp sunflower or rapeseed oil

¼ tsp black mustard seeds

10 curry leaves

½ tsp cumin seeds

2 whole red chillies, cut into
1 cm (½ in) pieces

2 onions, thinly sliced

6–8 garlic cloves, chopped

¼ tsp ground turmeric

salt to taste

few drops lime juice to taste

1 tbsp coriander (cilantro)
leaves, chopped

½ coconut, freshly grated or 100 g
(3½ oz/generous 1 cup) desiccated
(shredded) coconut
20–30 long, slender okra
(ladies' fingers)
salt to taste
¼ tsp ground turmeric
2 large green chillies, seeded, if liked,
and finely chopped
1–2 tbsp chopped coriander (cilantro)
leaves
½ tsp coriander seeds, finely crushed
but not to a powder
½ tsp cumin seeds, finely crushed
but not to a powder
2 tsp chaat masala
3–4 tbsp sunflower
or rapeseed oil

To serve
plain Greek-style yoghurt

BHARELI BHINDI

STUFFED OKRA

Serves 4

This recipe varies from place to place but this is a version that I feel works very well indeed as a lovely starter or accompaniment. Make sure you dry the okra (ladies' fingers) well after washing or they will become very gooey when you start to prepare them as they are naturally mucilaginous. Avoid thick, seedy-looking specimens as they will not become tender when cooked.

If using desiccated coconut, soak in 100 ml (3½ fl oz/scant ½ cup water) for 1 hour until soft and rehydrated and the liquid is absorbed.

Split the washed and dried okra lengthways, but not right through, and season inside with a little salt and the turmeric.

Blend the coconut and the remaining ingredients except the oil together and season lightly.

Stuff the okra until they are swollen but do not let them tear (don't worry if there is a little stuffing left over).

Heat just enough oil to cover the base of a heavy frying pan and fry the stuffed vegetables until golden brown on both sides and the okra are tender. Alternatively, grease an oven-proof tray, lay the okra (stuffed side up), brush lightly with some oil and bake in the oven at a temperature of 140°C/284°F/gas 1, for 15 minutes. Sprinkle over any remaining stuffing and serve with thick yoghurt.

CHOLE PINDI

NORTH INDIAN-STYLE CHICKPEAS

Serves 4–6

(see image on page 142)

A traditional Punjabi chickpea (garbanzo) dish which may vary from place to place and house to house but the method is more or less standard.

In the Punjab and Pakistan it is always served at ceremonies and on festive occasions. Punjabi ladies, please forgive my style!

If using dried, soaked chickpeas, wash them and place in a saucepan with plenty of water. Bring to the boil and boil rapidly for 10 minutes then reduce the heat slightly and cook until tender, up to 1 hour. Drain and set aside. You can also soak them for a few hours.

Heat the oil in a heavy-based pan and when a haze forms add the cumin seeds and sauté for 30 seconds until fragrant. Add the onion and sauté for 4–5 minutes until soft and golden. Stir in the garlic, ginger and green chillies and sauté for 3 minutes until lightly colouring. Lastly add the tomatoes and the yoghurt and stir in the chickpeas. Cook, stirring frequently, for a few minutes until the mixture is thoroughly heated, rich and thick.

Add the chaat or channa masala, if using. If not squeeze in a few drops of lemon juice. Stir in the coriander. Taste and adjust the seasoning.

Season and enjoy as part of a thali with warm flour tortillas or freshly-made chapattis or pooris.

200 g (7 oz/scant 1 cup) dried
chickpeas, soaked (or use
2 x 425 g cans, drained)
2–3 tbsp sunflower or
rapeseed oil
2 tsp cumin seeds, crushed
1 onion, finely chopped
5–6 garlic cloves, finely chopped
2.5 cm (1 in) piece of fresh ginger,
chopped
2–3 green chillies, split lengthways
2 tomatoes, chopped
60 ml (2 fl oz/¼ cup) plain,
Greek-style, whole milk yoghurt
1 tsp chaat or channa masala,
or a few drops of lemon juice
2 tbsp chopped coriander
(cilantro) leaves
salt to taste

To serve
warm flour tortillas,
or chapattis (see pages 183 or 85)
or pooris (see page 180 or 189)

3 x 250 g (9 oz) blocks paneer

a little melted butter or oil for basting

vegetable oil for deep-frying

For the marinade

2–3 heaped tbsp chickpea (garbanzo)
    or besan flour (optional)

6–8 sprigs of coriander (cilantro),
    roughly chopped

2–3 sprigs of mint, leaves picked

2–3 green chillies, seeded, if liked

10 cm (4 in) piece fresh ginger,
    roughly chopped

3–4 garlic cloves

¾ tsp garam masala

juice of ½ lime

½ tsp ground turmeric

2–3 tbsp sunflower or rapeseed oil
    (use some of the cooking oil, if liked)

salt to taste

oil for frying

To serve

boiled or vegetable rice (see pages 195
    and 199) and warm naan bread

HARIYALI PANNER

CHARGRILLED PANEER
IN GREEN MASALA

Serves 4–5

Recipes vary for this particular tikka like no other. Mothers, chefs and other cooks all claim that theirs is the best. I claim no such thing, but this recipe works for me. I've given you two options for cooking it. One fries the paneer (Indian whey) first, the other simply marinates it raw. Try both and find out which suits you.

Good quality paneer is available in most local supermarkets. It usually comes in 250 g (9 oz) blocks. The marinade makes enough for 4 slabs but you could reduce the quantity to make less. Best to start the marinating a day before or at least in the morning for an evening grilling or barbequing.

Cut each block of paneer into 6 rectangles – or small pieces if you prefer.

Heat the oil for deep-frying to 180°C (350°F), or until a cube of day-old bread dropped into the oil browns in 30 seconds.

Keep a large bowl half filled with warm to hot water in it on the side of the cooker and a colander over a separate bowl.

Deep-fry the paneer quickly in batches until lightly golden. Remove with a slotted spoon, place in the colander to drain off any excess oil and then straight into the water to soak. Alternatively, you can marinate the paneer straight from the packet. In restaurant kitchens we prefer to fry it first as it gives the paneer a better body and is easier to skewer and chargrill. The option is yours but you can try both methods in one go: simply fry half the paneer and leave half uncooked.

If using chickpea flour, toast it gently in a small, dry frying pan, stirring all the time with a wooden spatula over a low heat for 3–4 minutes until the colour changes slightly and it smells toasted. Do not allow to burn.

Tip the flour into a blender or food processor. Add all the remaining marinade ingredients and purée until smooth, adding a splash of water – but not too much – and stopping and scraping down the sides as necessary. Taste and check the seasoning. Tip into a sealable container.

Pat the paneer dry on paper towels, if fried. Squeeze each piece between your flattened palms, gently but firmly, and add to the marinade. Turn to coat completely. Seal and refrigerate for several hours, or overnight if more convenient.

Rub the bars of the grill (broiler) rack with oil, then heat the grill to high. Place the paneer pieces close together but not touching. Ideally brush them with a little melted butter or oil. Grill until browned on each side (2–3 minutes).

You can also barbecue the paneer skewers. Take two skewers and skewer the pieces of paneer at either end, by this I mean two skewers into each piece so that you can have three or four pieces per pair of skewers (depending on the size of the skewers). This makes grilling and turning them over easier as when the paneer becomes soft it is difficult to flip over. Alternatively, use a hinged barbecue rack to hold the slices firmly in a single layer. Try not to place the paneer on the rack directly over the coals as it is likely to stick.

Serve the paneer with rice, or as an accompaniment, or just on their own. Squeeze a little lime juice over before serving if you like.

PANEER BHURJEE

STIR-FRIED SPICED MINCED PANEER

Serves 4

A *Bhurjee* is a stir-fry of minced or finely chopped ingredients such as paneer, eggs or chicken. This makes a delicious quick meal for any time of day and can be made with a firm paneer cheese, crumbled feta or finely chopped halloumi.

2 tbsp sunflower or rapeseed oil

1 tbsp chopped garlic

1 tbsp chopped fresh ginger

1–2 green chillies, seeded, if liked, and chopped

1 heaped tsp cumin seeds, crushed

2 smallish onions, chopped

¼ tsp ground turmeric

½ tsp chilli powder

2 tomatoes, chopped

400 g (14 oz) paneer, minced or very finely chopped

salt to taste

1½ tbsp chopped coriander (cilantro) leaves

½ tsp chaat masala

To serve

chapattis (see pages 183 and 185) or naan or a pea pulao and some sweet chutney

Heat the oil in a flameproof casserole or heavy-based frying pan over a medium heat and add the chopped garlic, ginger and green chillies.

When the garlic begins to colour, add the cumin, stir for about 30 seconds until fragrant and then add the onions. Sauté for about 5 minutes until soft and lightly golden.

Add the turmeric and chilli powder, increase the heat and add the tomatoes. Sauté, taking care the mixture doesn't stick, for a further 2–3 minutes until the tomato juice has almost evaporated.

Reduce the heat to medium once again and gently fold in the paneer. Sauté until well heated and almost dry.

When heated through add salt and check seasoning, mix in the fresh coriander, remove from the heat, sprinkle with the chaat masala and serve with chapattis or other bread, or a pea pulao and some sweet chutney.

TADKA DAAL

SIZZLED LENTILS

Serves 4

(see page 142 for image)

Daal is the mainstay for a large proportion of the Indian population. In fact seventy-five to eighty per cent of households make some type of it in their homes daily! Daal is that one thing which even the poorest can afford to make and it is wholesome and filling. There are hundreds of daal recipes of which this is, perhaps, the most popular. You can also sizzle a spoonful of black mustard seeds and raw channa daal (yellow split peas) along with the other spices in the tadka for a different flavour. Try it another time.

250 g (9 oz/1 cup) red lentils (masoor daal)

250 g (9 oz/1⅓ cups) yellow lentils (toor daal)

1 tsp ground turmeric

salt to taste

50 g (2 oz/½ stick) butter

100 ml (3½ fl oz/scant ½ cup) sunflower or rapeseed oil

1 tsp cumin seeds

2 green chillies, split lengthways

1–2 dried red chillies, broken into pieces

5–6 garlic cloves

good pinch of ground asafoetida (optional)

Mix the 2 lentils in a deep bowl and wash them thoroughly in plenty of cold water, stirring them round, draining and refreshing the water repeatedly until it is almost clear.

Now soak them in plenty of fresh cold water for 5–6 hours. When the lentils have almost doubled in size you can boil them.

Tip them with their water in a deep pan to allow for expansion and add more water to come to 4 cm (1½ in) above the level of the lentils. Add the turmeric and a little salt. Bring to the boil stirring slowly from time to time so as not to let the lentils stick to the bottom of the pan. Skim the surface of scum if necessary. Add the butter when the scum has ceased. Simmer until the lentils are porridge-like and have absorbed most of the water, about 25 minutes.

When the lentils are cooked, remove from the heat. If liked, purée with a hand blender (but this isn't strictly necessary).

Heat the oil in a deep frying pan or a wok. When it is almost at smoking point add the cumin, chillies and garlic. Stir and cook until the garlic is golden in colour but not dark brown. Add the asafoetida, if using, as soon as the garlic is ready and remove from the heat.

Pour the contents of the pan in one go on to the lentils and stir well (it will sizzle and steam so keep your face away whilst doing this). Taste and re-season if necessary. Serve straight away, or cool quickly and store in the refrigerator. You will need to add a little water when reheating.

1 bunch of asparagus,
about 350 g (12 oz)
100 g (3½ oz/scant ½ cup) yellow split
peas, soaked for several hours
or overnight
1–2 tbsp sunflower or rapeseed oil
½ tsp black mustard seeds
½ tsp cumin seeds
2 tbsp freshly grated or desiccated
(shredded) coconut
6–8 curry leaves (preferably fresh),
finely shredded
salt to taste

ASPARAGUS PORIYAL

ASPARAGUS STIR-FRY

Serves 4

A simple yet tasty recipe that makes the most
of the short asparagus season. It is equally great
with winter squash – particularly pumpkin –
swede (rutabaga), turnips or kohl rabi when local
asparagus is not around.

Cut off about 6 cm (2½ in) from the bottom of the asparagus spears and set
aside to use for soup or trim bases, peel thinly, cut in two and blanch in boiling
water for 1–2 minutes to use in this dish too. Cut the remaining asparagus spears
into 2.5 cm (1 in) lengths.

Drain the soaked yellow split peas, rinse and drain well again.

Heat the oil in a heavy-based frying pan until a haze forms. Reduce the heat,
add the mustard seeds and cover with a lid until the crackling subsides.

Immediately add the cumin seeds, stir for a few seconds, add the yellow split
peas and sauté until well coated in the oil and the peas no longer stick to the pan.

Add the grated coconut and curry leaves and scrape the pan well with a wooden
spatula until the coconut has that beautiful toasted aroma.

Add the asparagus pieces, sauté for a minute or two and season to taste.

Good quality asparagus will cook within seconds and actually need not be
cooked well at all, just until hot through, it is that tender. Serve straight away.

MASALA NA PAPETA

SPICED POTATOES

Serves 4

The Parsees love for potato has brought about the creation of several dishes either of potato in its own right, or as an addition to meats and other vegetables.

In my eyes, Pervin and my mother-in-law make this dish the best and it has become one of our family favourites. It's simply delicious served as an accompaniment to meats, poultry and fried fish.

Par-boil the potatoes in just enough water to cover them for 5–6 minutes. Drain and set aside.

Heat the oil in a frying pan and add the cumin seeds. Allow the cumin to sizzle for about 30 seconds until fragrant.

Add the turmeric and the chilli powder and add the part-cooked potatoes. Reduce the heat and cover the pan. Cook gently, turning the contents from time to time until the potatoes are tender but still hold their shape.

Sprinkle over the lemon juice and mix well. Season to taste with salt and serve hot.

2 large potatoes, diced
2 tbsp sunflower or rapeseed oil
½ tsp cumin seeds
¼ tsp ground turmeric
½ tsp chilli powder
1 tsp lemon juice
salt to taste

PHOOL GOBI AUR MAKKI KAY DANEY

CAULIFLOWER FLORETS WITH SWEETCORN

Serves 4

In Rajasthan to accompany this as a light snack meal – and many other dishes – corn tortillas are made soft so that they can be eaten along with the food in the same way we eat chapattis. In North India, where corn grows in abundance, many different breads are made from corn, including crisp corn papadums, for instance.

To remove fresh corn kernels from the cobs, peel off the husks and trim the bases. Hold firmly upright on a board and slice down with a sharp knife. Repeat until all the corn is removed. They should yield about 100 g (3½ oz/½ cup) per cob.

Toast the cumin and coriander seeds in a dry frying pan for about 30 seconds until fragrant. Roughly crush in a mortar with a pestle (or in a small bowl with the end of a rolling pin). Set aside.

Sauté the onion in the oil over a medium heat for 2–3 minutes until just beginning to colour. Add the ginger and garlic paste and the chillies and sauté for 2 minutes. Add the crushed coriander and cumin and sauté for a further minute or two. Add the corn kernels and sauté for 1 minute.

Add the cauliflower florets and sauté for a further 4–5 minutes. Add the water and some salt and simmer until the florets are half cooked. Do not overcook the cauliflower.

Add the tomatoes and allow to soften for a minute or two.

When the desired texture for the cauliflower is reached, beat the yoghurt in a bowl with a fork or a small whisk until smooth and add. Simmer for 4–5 minutes until you get a creamy-looking rich sauce.

Check the seasoning and add the coriander. Stir and remove from the heat.

Serve as a side dish or with corn tortillas.

1 tsp cumin seeds

2 tsp coriander seeds

1 onion, chopped

3 tbsp sunflower or
rapeseed oil

1 tbsp ginger and garlic paste
(see page 157) or use 3 garlic cloves,
crushed and 1 tsp grated
fresh ginger

2 green chillies, seeded,
if liked, and chopped

200 g (7 oz/1 cup) young, fresh or
thawed, frozen sweetcorn kernels

1 small cauliflower, cut into
small florets

120 ml (4 fl oz/ ½ cup) water

salt to taste

2 tomatoes, chopped

2–3 heaped tbsp plain
Greek-style yoghurt

2 tbsp chopped coriander
(cilantro) leaves

To serve

corn tortillas

500 ml (17 fl oz/2 ¼ cups) Greek-style
plain yoghurt

2 tbsp sunflower or rapeseed oil

½ tsp black mustard seeds

10–15 curry leaves, preferably fresh

1 tsp cumin seeds

¼ tsp ground asafoetida

3 tbsp chickpea (garbanzo) or besan
flour, sifted

½ tsp ground turmeric

2–3 green chillies, split lengthways
and seeded

1 tbsp caster (superfine)
sugar

salt to taste

150 ml (5 fl oz/⅔ cup) water

1 tbsp chopped coriander (cilantro)
leaves

To serve

Boiled rice (see page 195) or khichdi
(see page 200)

Clockwise: naan, Sizzled Lentils (page 133) cucumber raita, North Indian-Style Chickpeas (page 126), Boiled Rice (page 195), Spiced-Onion Fritters (page 163).
Centre: Yoghurt Curry (opposite).

DAHI NI KADHI

YOGHURT CURRY

Serves 6

This is a basic, simple Kadhi how my mother made it, though different regions of India have they own ways of making it. It is perfect plain, but myriad items can be added and simmered in the curry at the end to give it more complexity: fried, thinly sliced okra (ladies' fingers) or aubergine (eggplant) pieces; small onion or cauliflower fritters (page 163); thickly sliced raw banana or fried plantain. You can even drink it hot with your food.

Beat the yoghurt in a bowl with a whisk and set aside.

Heat the oil in a heavy-based pan until it forms a haze. Add the mustard seeds and, when they stop crackling, add the curry leaves and the cumin. Stir over a medium heat for a minute without allowing the cumin to burn. Add the asafoetida. Remove from the heat and slowly mix in the chickpea flour, stirring all the time to avoid any lumps forming.

When well mixed return to a low heat and cook the flour, stirring with a wooden spoon, until it releases the oil and becomes soft (in the beginning the flour will absorb all the oil and become firm and hard, but with slow cooking and stirring, it will gradually soften and then release the oil).

When soft, add the turmeric and the green chillies and cook, stirring, for a minute·or two. Remove from the heat, allow to cool for a few minutes, then add the whisked yoghurt and mix thoroughly to a smooth paste. Blend in the water and return to the heat. Bring to the boil over a medium heat. Add the sugar and salt to taste. It should be a bit sour but also a bit sweet and savoury.

Boil, stirring continuously, for a few minutes until thickened to the consistency of a cream soup. Add the coriander and serve with plain rice or khichdi.

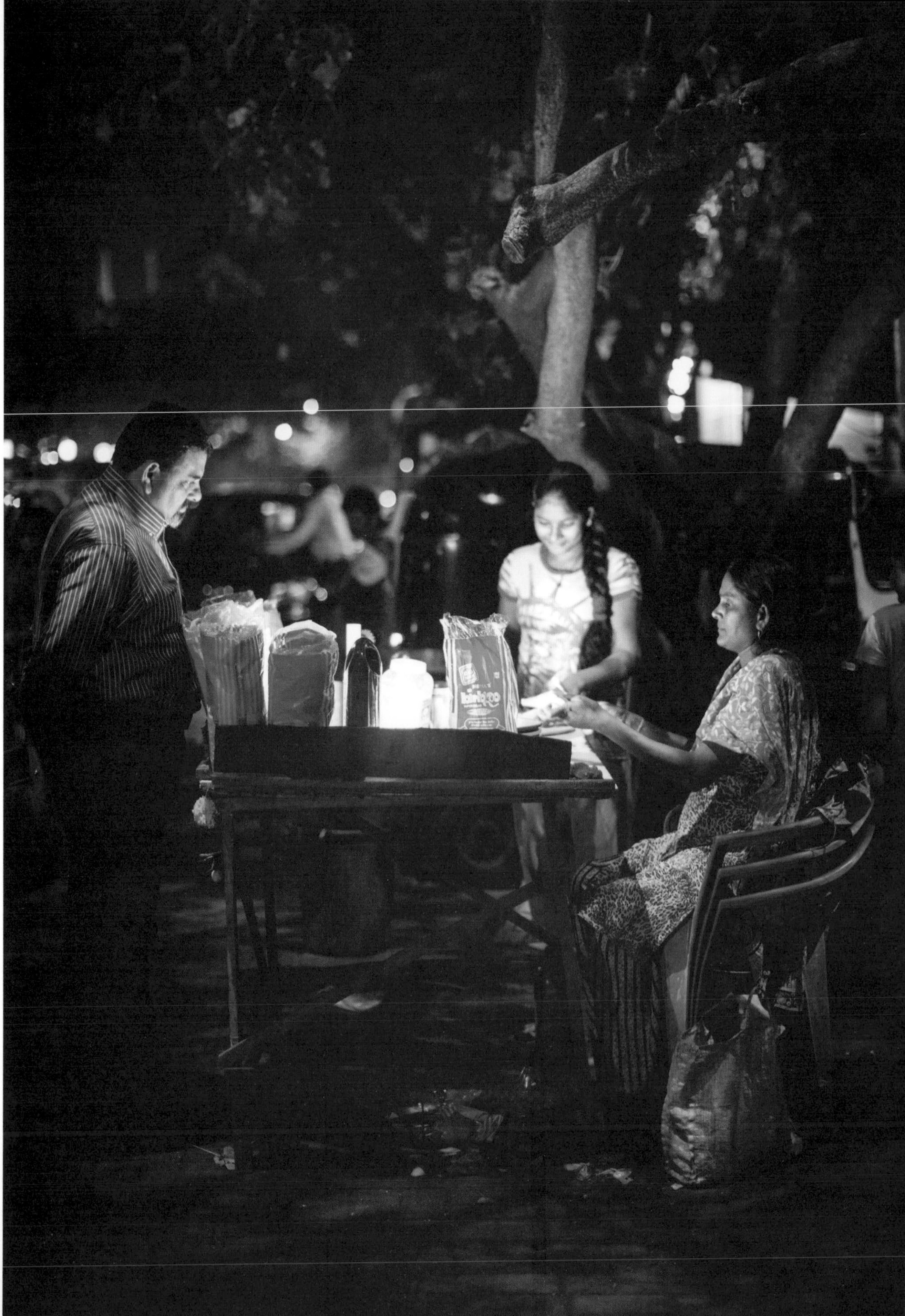

STREET FOOD

If one city in India is truly reflective of the vast array of the subcontinents' street food extravaganza, then it has got to be Bombay/Mumbai!

Bombay's street food is unrivalled and can satisfy any budget from the poorest of the poor to the rich and famous, the high and mighty and the Hoity-Toity, all of whom indulge in the street delights of this magnificent city, which was our home for years and still feels like home every time we go back.

You might be surprised that a famous place like Baday Miyas whose *Baida Roti* (page 148) is legendary and has been on the streets ever since I began my career at the Taj in 1975, attracts the richest of the rich in their flashy Rollers and fancy Ferraris, jostling with the poor and foodies like us to get in first.

If a Juicewalla gets famous because of a cocktail of juices he has perfected, rest assured there will be lines of cars waiting to be served until the wee hours of the morning, which may sound baffling.

Likewise, our local Good Luck restaurant, which I have been frequenting since the late sixties as a very young lad (from when proper pocket money kicked in to now) is where we go every time we are in Bombay to satisfy our passion for their *Kheema Ghotala* (page 157) which simply translates as 'Confused Mince'. The place has changed little, and despite all the mobile phones and hi-tech devices in everyone's hands, the people and their attitudes towards Good Luck's food haven't changed either.

The Great Bombay Street Sandwich (see pages 158–9) draws the foodies to their own favourites. Bombayites will travel fifty miles to eat what they love from a particular vendor for a 20-rupee sandwich. That's how mad and dedicated our people are when it comes to good food! A delicious, tasty meal can be bought with loose change, and is worth travelling for miles to get to. In our rather mad days we would drive twenty-strong on motorbikes for a hundred kilometres outside Bombay just to eat a famous biryani from a little roadside shack. That's crazy considering you have to ride back after a heavy meal.

But Bombaywallas still do these and will go a long way to get 'That man's famous onion bhajias' or 'this guy's fish koliwada' or 'That fellow's *bhael poori*' or 'That lady's *wada pao*'. That is passion and commitment and no doubt a sheer urge to satisfy that craving the palate demands.

Street food also came with the usual haunts of the 'Booze Aunties'! All of us knew of at least two or three places where we could buy an out-of-hours tipple. It was either Aunty Josephine or Aunty Mary or Aunty Cecelia, but we never saw their faces. Money and little bottles were always exchanged from behind a curtain: a hand would come out and take your money, a little opening in the curtain again meant change and the goods were thrust out. We were all victims of a little alcoholic desire, and the only thing dictating whether we bought cheap locally distilled booze or a slightly upmarket rum was the size of our pockets.

No matter what your tastebuds call for, or for that matter how much money you have at your disposal, Bombay will amaze you, astound you, excite you and leave you spellbound if you take the decision to be adventurous and pig out. That is a guarantee!

BAIDA ROTI

EGG ROTI PARCEL

Serves 5–8

Baida is egg for Bombayites and *roti*, of course, is the famous flattened unleavened bread. This pan-fried, folded chapatti-style one can be stuffed with several different fillings. This favourite street food is sold in several parts of Bombay, but originated at the famous Baday Miya – hence its name. Baday Miya is situated in Colaba in a byway behind the Taj Mahal Hotel. It opened soon after we had started working at the Taj and has now become somewhat of a Bombay institution. Its street-side kebabs and Baida Roti attract thousands of locals as well as visitors and tourists to Bombay who yearn for a taste of this famous eatery. Baday Miya only operates in the evenings. This is not its actual recipe but it will give you an idea of what you could experience there. Adjust the chilli according to taste. You can use plain flour tortillas or ready-made chapattis but we thought you might like to try your hand at making these simple rotis from scratch. So here goes!

First make the roti. Sift the flour, salt and baking powder into a bowl. Form a well in the centre and break the egg into it. Gradually work the egg into the flour and add the oil. Mix with just enough water to form a soft but not sticky dough. Knead briefly until smooth. Divide into 5 to 8 equal portions and roll into round balls. Keep the dough covered with damp cloth and set aside for approximately an hour.

Meanwhile make the filling. Sauté the onions in the oil in a frying pan for about 5 minutes until golden. Add the ginger, garlic and green chillies and continue to sauté until the garlic is lightly golden.

Add the meat (if using mutton make sure it is lean and well trimmed) and fry over a medium heat, stirring until cooked through and all the grains of meat are separate, adding a little water if necessary, to prevent burning.

Add the garam masala and herbs and season to taste with salt.

Beat the eggs with a pinch of salt but not too much as both the roti and the mince have salt.

Roll out each ball of the roti dough into a thin square shape.

Heat a non-stick frying pan and place a roti on it.

Divide the meat mixture into the same amount of portions as the roti dough. Put a portion of the meat in the centre of the roti in the pan, flatten it slightly and pour two tablespoons of beaten egg over the mince.

Fold in the edges to make a square packet that can hold the mince and egg in.

Spoon a little more beaten egg over and drizzle a little oil.

Gently turn it over and pour a little more of the beaten egg so that the roti parcel is covered with egg on all sides. Gently fry over a low heat, adding more oil if necessary, until all the sides are golden and crisp. Remove from the pan and keep warm whilst making the remainder.

Serve hot with green chutney or, as we Bombaywallas often like, ketchup as well!

For the rotis

250 g (9 oz/2¼ cups) plain
(all-purpose) flour

½ tsp salt

¼ tsp baking powder

1 tbsp vegetable oil

1 egg

For the filling

2 small onions, finely chopped

2 tbsp vegetable or rapeseed oil

7.5 cm (3 in) piece of fresh ginger,
finely chopped

4–6 garlic cloves,
finely chopped

2 green chillies,
chopped (seeded, if preferred)

400 g (14 oz/1¾ cups) lean minced
(ground) lamb or mutton

¾ tsp garam masala

2 tbsp chopped coriander (cilantro)
leaves

1 tbsp chopped mint leaves

salt, to taste

6–8 eggs, beaten

To serve

Fresh Green Chutney (see page 215)
or ketchup (catsup)

For the filling

500 g (1 lb 2 oz) lean, boneless lamb, cut in 1 cm (½ in) dice

2 tbsp sunflower or rapeseed oil

2 onions, very finely chopped

2 tbsp ginger and garlic paste (see page 157), or use

5–6 garlic cloves, crushed and

1 tbsp grated fresh ginger

1 tbsp ground coriander

1 tsp ground cumin

1 tbsp red chilli paste

salt to taste

60–75 ml (2–2½ fl oz/ ¼ – ⅓ cup) thick, plain yoghurt

1–2 tomatoes, chopped (optional)

1 tbsp lemon juice

1 tbsp chopped mint leaves

2 tbsp chopped coriander (cilantro) leaves

1 tsp garam masala

For the egg roti

2 eggs

chilli powder (optional)

sunflower oil, ghee or butter for frying

6 small flour tortillas or plain flour chapattis

1–2 onions, thinly sliced

2 tsp chopped coriander (cilantro) leaves

12–18 mint leaves, shredded or snipped with scissors

MUMBAI NO FRANKIE

BOMBAY LAMB WRAP

Serves 3–6

This was once Bombay's hot selling (non-vegetarian) street snack until it was overcome by modern American junk food but this stuffed, rolled chapatti is still a favourite with many. The egg roti can be eaten separately from the meat as part of a main course, or, as here, made into a snack to eat on the go. To make your own red chilli paste, soak dried red chillies in a little water, until they become swollen and soft. Snip into pieces with scissors. Purée in a clean coffee grinder or small food processor. Place in a clean screw-topped jar and cover with a thin layer of sunflower oil to prevent air getting to it. Store in the refrigerator.

First make the filling. Wash and drain the lamb well in a colander.

Heat the oil in a flameproof casserole or heavy-based saucepan and brown the lamb quickly on all sides. Stir often enough so that all sides get evenly browned and the meat is dry.

Add the chopped onions, the ginger and garlic paste, ground coriander, cumin and chilli paste.

Sauté until the onions and the masala start to brown and get a rich dark colour.

Keep scraping the bottom as you go along with a flat wooden spatula to prevent sticking and burning. Add a little water if necessary. The addition of water will also help to prevent the spices from burning as well as aid more even colouring and cooking.

Check the salt and add as desired.

Lower the heat and cover the pan. Cook for 30 minutes then stir in the yoghurt and tomatoes, if using, cover and continue to cook for about 30 minutes or until the lamb is really tender and bathed in a rich, thick sauce.

When the lamb is cooked add the lemon juice, the mint, coriander and garam masala. Taste and re-season, if necessary. Cover and set aside. Later you may like to remove any excess oil floating on the top with a tablespoon and save it for future use in other lamb dishes. Reheat just before serving.

To make the Frankies: beat the eggs well and add 2 tablespoons of water. Add a pinch of salt and, if you like, a pinch of chilli powder. Heat a little oil, butter or ghee in a frying pan, tava or griddle pan over a medium heat. Swirl round (there should be just enough to coat the pan). Pour off excess. Add a tortilla or chapatti to the pan and pour a little egg on the top, enough to just coat the surface. You may like to brush the egg on instead though the Indians definitely prefer a thicker coating of egg. The omelette-like taste of the chapatti enhances the flavour of the Frankie.

As soon as you see the egg coagulating flip it over and coat the other side. Then flip again.

When both sides are golden brown remove on to a plate and keep warm. Wipe out the pan, add a little more oil, butter or ghee, reheat then repeat the whole wiping, greasing and cooking process with the remaining breads and egg.

Place one tablespoon of the lamb, or more if required, along one side of an egg roti. Sprinkle with sliced onion, chopped coriander and mint, and roll up. Repeat with the remaining rotis and lamb and serve.

100 g (3½ oz/ scant ½ cup) yellow split
peas (channa daal) soaked for several
hours in cold water, then drained
and dried
1 cm (½ in) piece of fresh ginger,
roughly chopped
3 garlic cloves
10 mint leaves
100 g (3½ oz) paneer
1 large floury potato, boiled,
peeled and mashed
1 small red onion, grated or
finely chopped
1 tbsp chopped coriander (cilantro)
leaves
1 small green chilli, seeded,
if liked, and finely chopped
½ tsp ground cumin
1 tsp lime juice
½ tsp chaat masala
a little chickpea (garbanzo) or
besan flour
15–20 young spinach leaves,
finely shredded
salt and coarsely crushed black pepper
vegetable oil for deep-frying

To serve
sliced fresh tomatoes or
Fresh Green Chutney (see page 215)

ALOO PANEER AUR CHANNA PAKORA

FRIED INDIAN CHEESE WITH POTATOES & YELLOW SPLIT PEAS

Make 40–50

An interesting little street food item, made with nutritious channa daal (yellow split peas) which is ideal for a starter, a midday snack or for afternoon tea. Chaat masala is available from Indian stores and some supermarkets. Try haloumi or feta if you cannot get paneer but they are saltier. Other cheeses that give a good flavour are strong cheddar or red Leicester.

Blitz the split peas, ginger, garlic and mint together in a food processor until the mixture has the consistency of coarse breadcrumbs. Add the paneer and process again. Tip into a bowl.

Stir in the mashed potato, chopped onion, chopped coriander, the green chilli, cumin, lime juice and chaat masala.

Mix to a soft dough with a little chickpea flour, a spoonful at a time.

Lastly add the shredded spinach leaves and mix them in gently, then season with a little salt and some coarsely crushed black pepper.

Heat the oil for deep-frying. Take a tiny bit of the mixture and fry until golden. Drain on paper towels then check the seasoning and correct, if necessary.

Shape the dough into 40–50 small balls and deep-fry a few at a time, so as not to cool the oil too rapidly, until golden brown. Drain on paper towels. Reheat the oil between batches and keep the balls warm whilst cooking the remainder.

Serve with fresh tomato or green chutney.

½ tsp ground turmeric

1 tsp chilli powder

2 tsp ground coriander

1 tsp ground cumin

1 tsp garam masala

200 ml (7 fl oz/scant 1 cup) water

3 tbsp vegetable or rapeseed oil

2 tbsp ginger and garlic paste,
    (see recipe tip), or 5–6 garlic cloves,
    crushed and 1 tbsp grated fresh ginger

4–5 green chillies, seeded, if liked
    and chopped

2 onions, chopped

500 g (1 lb 2 oz/2 ¼ cups) minced
    (ground) lamb, mutton or goat

juice of ½ lime

salt to taste

1 tbsp chopped coriander (cilantro) leaves

1 tbsp chopped mint leaves

4 eggs, beaten

KHEEMA GHOTALA

CURRIED MINCED MEAT SCRAMBLED WITH EGG

Serves 4–6

I am not sure it is possible to write any book on Bombay's great cuisine culture and not include a kheema dish, whether it be eaten with soft rolls, bread or chapatti, or baked covered in mashed potato as a cottage pie. You can also add a couple of chopped tomatoes or add 3 tablespoons tomato ketchup (catsup) and cook until well blended and the minced meat takes on a rich sheen.

Alternatively try our very own breakfast favourite *Kheema Ghotala*. It might sound strange to eat mince for breakfast but in Bombay this is a common delicacy. Heat levels differ and we always blend ours with bits of chopped green chilli which you can then pick out but the flavour remains. Just for interest, mutton is a general word in India for lamb, mutton or goat.

Tip: If you cook a lot of Indian dishes, you could make a jar of garlic and ginger paste: simply peel a good-sized piece of fresh ginger and an equal volume of garlic cloves. Purée in a blender with a splash of water to form a smooth paste. Pack into a clean screw-topped jar, cover with a little sunflower or rapeseed oil to keep out the air, seal and store in the refrigerator. When you use some, re-cover with oil each time.

Blend the spices with the water in a small bowl, cover and set aside.

Heat a heavy-based saucepan, add the oil and, when a haze forms, add the garlic and ginger and the green chilli and sauté, stirring well with a wooden spatula to prevent sticking at the bottom.

Once the paste colours lightly and becomes fragrant (but take care not to let it burn), add the onions and sauté until golden over a medium heat. Add a little water to deglaze the pan. Continue to sauté the onions adding water every now and again over a medium to low heat until the onions are very soft and pulpy.

Now add the soaked spices (rinse out the bowl with a little more water and add that too) and sauté until you see the oil emerge, you might need to add a little water again to prevent sticking.

Remove from the heat and add the mince. Work it in well with the spatula until it is totally broken up and blended very well into the masala. Return to the heat and cook stirring regularly until the meat is cooked and all the meat grains are separate.

Season and stir in the lime juice and herbs. The kheema can now be served as suggested in the introduction or, for our breakfast dish, it's time to add the ghotala which also, incidentally, means 'confusion'. Simply pour the beaten eggs into the cooked kheema and stir gently over the heat until they are scrambled to your liking, but take care not to let it boil or the eggs will curdle. We like ours soft as it makes for a great filling in a soft breakfast roll but some prefer to cook it without stirring much, so the eggs set like an omelette. Either way the taste is superb and you will enjoy it!

VEGETABLE SANDWICH

THE GREAT BOMBAY STREET SANDWICH

Makes 4 sandwiches

This is some sandwich, and the recipe varies from stall owner to stall owner. To have it plain, toasted, grilled (broiled) or griddled is entirely the customer's choice here. In fact, in Bombay we used to get an option for butter too. One was a margarine-type homogenized spread known as Rita Butter and the other, of course, proper butter.

For the filling, everything here can be optional but this is our favourite combination. A word about the onions: we Indians simply love them raw, though in the West people are more worried about 'onion breath', which we seldom worry about, so you may wish to use less than we suggest. Beetroot (red beet) is also optional but gives great colour, texture and taste.

The bread of Bombay is also a famous part of this sandwich and is a unique-sized loaf, smaller than European loaves. A medium-sized slice of Western bread is the best alternative for this.

First mix all the masala ingredients together in a small bowl. Place in a salt or pepper shaker, if liked (or you can just sprinkle it by hand when the time comes).

Next make the chutney. Blitz all the ingredients in a blender or small food processor.

Now for the sandwich. Butter the bread, then smear the hot mint chutney over. Top 4 slices with sliced beetroot then potato, then top with another slice of buttered chutneyed bread. Sprinkle with some masala, then another buttered slice. Layer onion, tomato and cucumber on this. Sprinkle with more masala and the final slices of bread, chutney sides down.

Press down and either cut each sandwich into quarters and serve or toast in a sandwich toaster, under a grill (broiler) or on a griddle and serve hot with tomato ketchup.

For a milder sandwich, omit the masala or just sprinkle a little on the finished sandwich.

You can make the sandwich with toasted bread instead of toasting it later but cooking it filled changes and intensifies the flavours.

For the masala

1 tsp salt

½ tsp chilli powder

1 tsp dried mango powder

½ tsp cumin seeds, toasted
and crushed

For the chutney

3–4 mint sprigs, leaves picked

4–5 coriander (cilantro) sprigs

1 thin green chilli, seeded, if liked,
and chopped

2 tsp caster (superfine) sugar

¾ tsp cumin seeds, toasted
and crushed

salt to taste

juice of ½ lime

For the sandwich

butter

12 medium soft white bread slices

1 cooked beetroot (red beet), sliced

2 large waxy potatoes, boiled,
peeled and sliced

3–4 beefsteak tomatoes

2 red onions, sliced

1 small cucumber, sliced

To serve

tomato ketchup (catsup),
if serving the sandwich toasted

2 onions, core removed, halved and very
   thinly sliced

2 green chillies, finely chopped
   or minced

1 tsp chilli powder

2 tbsp chopped coriander (cilantro) leaves

1 tsp cumin seeds, coarsely crushed

½ tsp ajwain (lovage) seeds, crushed

½ tsp ground turmeric

½ tsp lemon juice

40 g (1½ oz/⅓ cup) chickpea
   (garbanzo) or besan flour

½ tsp salt (or to taste)

2 tbsp water

vegetable oil for deep-frying

To serve

any of the fresh chutneys (see pages 212–219)

KAANDA BHAJIAS

SPICED ONION FRITTERS

Makes 20–30

This is perhaps the most popular and most common of all Indian snacks, but possibly the most misunderstood and wrongly made. What you see in stores and supermarkets does not always represent the bhajia we Indians know. The word *bhajia* simply means fritter and *bhaji* means either spinach or cooked vegetables. When you make these they will taste like those from an Indian home, or almost. They are very simple to prepare and the results will astound you.

Place the onions in a deep bowl and add all the ingredients except the chickpea flour, salt and water.

Sift the chickpea flour with the salt.

Start heating the oil for deep-frying.

Mix the flour and salt slowly into the onions and rub it in with your fingers, until the mix is firm and sticky. Try and use one palm only.

Add the water and mix further for a minute or two, check the salt and you are ready to fry.

The oil should be heated to 180°C (350°F) or until a tiny bit of the batter drops in, sizzles, rises to the surface and browns in 30 seconds. Do not have the oil too hot or they will fry too fast and remain raw inside and gooey. Too cold and the results will be oily and soft.

With your already-messy fingers put small dollops of the batter into the oil to fry. The bhajias should be no bigger than 2.5 cm (1 in) diameter. Fry a few at a time until crisp and golden – about 4 minutes – turning in the oil, if necessary. Do not put too many in the oil in one go or they will be pale and soggy as the oil temperature will drop too much. Reheat the oil between batches.

You can, on the other hand, if you want to serve them later, half-fry and remove them then briefly re-fry in very hot oil to brown and crisp when ready to serve. When cooked, remove with a slotted spoon and drain on paper towels. Serve the bhajias with any of the green chutneys or the fresh tomato and garlic chutney.

200 g (7 oz/generous 1 cup) sago
pearls (preferably large)
2 large floury potatoes, boiled,
peeled and mashed
3 heaped tbsp raw
skinned peanuts
1 tsp cumin seeds
2 green chillies, seeded if liked,
and finely chopped
1 tsp lime juice
salt to taste
1–2 tbsp chopped coriander (cilantro)
leaves
about 2 tbsp rice flour (optional)
vegetable oil for deep-frying

To serve
any chutney (see pages 212–219)
or tomato ketchup (catsup)

SABOODANA WADA

CRISPY FRIED SAGO & POTATO CAKES

Makes 12–14 cakes

Sago pearls are used quite extensively in various parts of India but none more so than in Maharashtra and in Southern India where most of the tapioca is also grown. Sago cakes taste great and are pretty addictive. Peanuts are best but if you are allergic then add cashew nuts. Sago is readily available in most supermarkets, though do try and purchase the large pearls instead of the tiny ones. An important tip: soaking time will depend on the quality, size and age of the sago pearls. Some smaller balls take only 15–20 minutes to soak well, expand and become soft, whilst some larger ones are best left overnight. We have used the larger pearls for this recipe.

Wash the sago as you would rice. Place in a bowl, just-cover with water and leave to soak for several hours or overnight until the water is absorbed, the pearls look plump and one feels soft when lifted out and crushed in the fingers. Drain the sago well in a colander for at least 15–20 minutes.

Meanwhile, dry-roast the peanuts in a frying pan, stirring, until light brown then coarsely chop by hand or in a food processor (but be careful not to grind too finely as the texture gives a delightful crunch to the Wadas).

Mix all the ingredients (except the rice flour) in a large bowl until well combined.

If the sago has been well drained the mixture should bind together to shape into cakes. But if too wet, add a little rice flour.

Dust your hands with rice flour and then shape the mixture into small cakes. Chill, for 30 minutes or more, until firm.

Heat the oil for deep-frying to 180°C (350°F) or until a cube of day-old bread browns in 30 seconds. Have a colander set over a bowl ready to drain the cakes. Do not place them on paper towel to drain or they may stick. Fry 2 or 3 at a time, turning once until golden on both sides. Drain in the colander and keep warm whilst cooking the remainder.

Serve with any fresh green chutney or ketchup even, as some Indians do.

BATATA WADA

SPICED POTATO FRITTERS OR BALLS

Makes 10–12

The veritable *Batata Wada* is a mainstay for thousands of Bombay's residents when it comes to an affordable midday filler. Many even start with a good Wada for breakfast. For my wife it is an absolute must to eat almost daily whenever we visit Bombay. The basic spiced potato and onion mix can be served three ways: as it is as an accompaniment with bread or chapattis (pages 183 or 185), made into potato bhajias, or, as here, made into Wadas.

Put the mashed potatoes into a large bowl, season and add the chopped coriander, then set aside.

Heat the 2 tablespoons of oil in a large frying pan (have a lid or a frying pan mesh to hand).

Add the mustard seeds, cover with the lid or mesh, reduce the heat and cook for 15–20 seconds, shaking the pan until they crackle and pop. Be careful not to burn the seeds.

As soon as the crackling dies a bit add the curry leaves and asafoetida and swirl round the pan.

Add the ginger and chilli and sauté for a minute or two then add the chopped onions. Sauté gently until the onions are pale and soft, then add the turmeric and the lime juice and add this mixture to the potatoes.

Mix well, taste and re-season if necessary.

Now to make the mixture into wadas. Sift the chickpea flour into a bowl and add enough water beating all the time with a whisk to make a smooth, creamy pouring batter the consistency of batter when frying fish or making pancakes. Season, cover and leave to stand for at least 30 minutes.

Beat the potato mixture well to make it as smooth as possible and shape into 10–12 equal-sized balls. If serving as a canapé snack, make the balls much smaller.

Heat the oil to 180°C/350°F or until a tiny dribble of the batter dropped in sizzles, rises to the surface immediately and browns in 30 seconds.

Fry all the Wadas a few at a time until crisp and golden, turning over if necessary. Remove with a slotted spoon and drain in a colander over a bowl, or on paper towels. Serve in soft rolls with fresh chutney.

4–5 floury potatoes, boiled, peeled and mashed

salt to taste

2 tbsp chopped coriander (cilantro) leaves

2 tbsp sunflower or rapeseed oil

1 tsp black mustard seeds

10–12 curry leaves (preferably fresh), chopped

¼ tsp ground asafoetida

7.5 cm (3 in) piece of fresh ginger, finely chopped

1–2 thin green chillies finely chopped, including the seeds

1–2 red onions, finely chopped

½ tsp ground turmeric

juice of ½ lime

250 g (9 oz/2 cups) chickpea (garbanzo) or besan flour

vegetable oil for deep-frying

To serve

soft rolls and any chutney (see pages 212–219)

TIKKHA MURGHI NA SAMOSA

JUMPING CHICKEN SAMOSA

Makes about 50

There is no Indian equivalent name – this is universal and very special. A samosa is simply a pastry filled with a variety of fillings, shaped into a triangle and deep-fried. Samosas vary across the length and breadth of the subcontinent. Every community has their own ways of making the fillings and pastry as well as added differences between the Muslim and Hindu variations. However a certain Memon gentlemen, Mr Ebrahim, used to visit Bombay's famous Juhu Beach every evening with a helper carrying a huge basket of hot, hot samosas. They were so hot with minced chillies that they literally made you jump. He was seen and heard shouting, 'Jumping chicken, chicken is jumping!' and people would throng and hundreds of the samosas would vanish in minutes. Job done, he would retire and the sugar cane juice man who he stood next to, would be thumping with business as people doused their mouths. I was told that Mr Ebrahim also owned the juice stall!

The word *tikkha* means 'chilli hot' (and is also used to refer to a woman with a fiery-hot temper!). Ours, of course, are milder than what you get in Bombay, but you can turn the spicing all the way up (or down) if you like. Use minced (ground) lamb, beef, venison, lean pork or game instead of chicken, too.

Note, if you buy dried wrappers, each one will have to be dipped in water before cutting and filling. You can cheat and use filo pastry if necessary.

Make sure you get all the ingredients prepared before you start.

Blend the turmeric, chilli and curry powders and the garam masala with 200 ml (7 fl oz/scant 1 cup) of the water. Beat this masala well with a spoon, cover and set aside.

Heat the oil in a wok or a flameproof casserole until you see a haze. Add the curry leaves and green chillies, then the cumin seeds. Stir for a few seconds until fragrant then add the ginger and garlic. Sauté until the garlic begins to change colour slightly then add the onions and sauté until soft but not brown, about 4 minutes. Stir and scrape the base of the casserole well with a flat wooden spatula to prevent sticking.

When the onions are soft add the prepared masala. Rinse out the masala bowl with a splash more water and add too. Cook, stirring for a few minutes, until the water has evaporated and the aroma is rich and not raw smelling.

Add the remaining 250 ml (8½ fl oz/1 cup) of water, remove the pan from the heat and add the mince. Blend well until it is smooth and fully blended with no lumps. Return to the heat, increase the heat and cook, stirring frequently until the mince is cooked through and most of the liquid has evaporated.

Add the peas and herbs and remove from the heat. If there is fat on the surface, strain the mixture through a sieve (strainer) to remove it. Taste and re-season, if necessary. Leave until cold.

Now to make the samosas. You must keep a damp cloth ready to cover the pastry as you work on the individual samosas. Place the stack of spring roll sheets on a board. Using a tea plate or large saucer as a guide, place on top and cut round it, using a sharp thin-tipped knife, through the entire stack to make round discs. The trimmings can be cut into small pieces, deep-fried and either eaten as they are, or mixed in a chaat, (see page 175) for added bite.

Continued overleaf

1 tsp ground turmeric

2 tsp chilli powder

1 heaped tbsp curry powder

2 tsp garam masala

450 ml (15 fl oz/2 cups) water

3 tbsp sunflower or rapeseed oil

30–40 curry leaves, preferably fresh,
finely shredded or chopped like parsley

8–10 thin green chillies, finely chopped

1 kg (2 lb 3 oz) minced
(ground) chicken

1 heaped tsp cumin seeds

100 g (3½ oz/½ cup) ginger and
garlic paste (see page 151), or use
50 g (2 oz) each of garlic cloves and
fresh ginger, crushed to a
paste together

4–5 small onions, finely chopped

500 g (1 lb 2 oz/3½ cups) fresh shelled
or frozen peas, blanched
for 2 minutes and drained

5–6 sprigs of mint, leaves picked
and finely shredded

2 tbsp chopped coriander (cilantro)

250 g packet (50 sheets) frozen small
spring roll wrappers, about
15 cm (6 in) square, thawed
(Singaporian or Malaysian are best)

2 tbsp plain (all-purpose) flour
for sealing

To serve

Fresh Green Chutney (see page 215)

TIKKA MURGHTI NA SAMOSA
JUMPING CHICKEN SAMOSA

Continued from previous page

Now cut the disc into half and keep one pile on top of the other. Cover with a damp cloth (and keep them covered all the time you are working on each samosa).

You will also need a sealant to stick the samosa edges together. Mix the flour with a little water until you have a porridge consistency.

Peel off the top 2 semicircular sheets (a single sheet is too thin for this and will not make a good samosa). Now taking one edge of the semicircle, fold it over to the centre and, applying a dab of flour paste with a pastry brush, stick the edge.

Then folding the other edge over make it into a cone, making sure the lower tip is fully sealed with no hole at the point. Seal that edge too.

Fill the cone to about 2 cm (¾ in) from the top.

Then fold one side of the top edge in over the filling apply a dab of the paste and fold the other edge over the top.

Rub your fingers over it a few times until you are sure the samosa is well sealed. Repeat until all the samosas are made.

Heat the oil for deep-frying to 180°C (350°F) or until a cube of day-old bread browns in 30 seconds and deep-fry the samosas until crisp and golden, about 3–4 minutes. Drain on paper towels and enjoy with fresh green chutney.

500 g (1 lb 2 oz) lean lamb
shoulder meat
20 g (¾ oz) bunch of
coriander (cilantro)
20 g (¾ oz) bunch of mint
2.5 cm (1 in) piece of fresh ginger,
roughly chopped
1 large green chilli
6–8 garlic cloves
1 tsp garam masala
1 tsp ground cumin
1 tsp ground coriander
½ tsp chilli powder
½ tsp ground turmeric
1 tsp lime juice
salt to taste
1 tsp vegetable oil

To serve
Fresh Green Chutney (see page 215),
kachumber (see page 93), and
chapattis (see pages 183 and 185), or
flour tortillas (optional)

SEEKH KAVÂAB

LAMB MINCE KEBAB

Serves 4

The literal translation of this dish is 'kebab formed on a skewer'. One of the many great representatives of Indian cuisine, *Seekh Kavâab*, or kebab as it is mostly called, is usually a street-side speciality.

A Muslim dish, which can be traced to its Persian roots, it also varies in recipe from state to state and region to region. This, perhaps, is the one which is appeals to most palates and is one of the simplest and best. Though the meat used should always be lean, a little fat will bring out the best flavour and a superb texture.

Clean the meat well, removing all sinews and gristle. Do not discard any fat if found.

Cut the meat into pieces small enough so as not to jam the mincer (grinder).

Mince (grind) all the ingredients together except the powdered spices, lime juice and salt. Alternatively grind the herbs and whole spices in a food processor to a paste then add the lamb and finely chop to the consistency of mince.

Once the meat is minced add the spice powders and lime juice and knead well.

To check the seasoning, if you do not like tasting raw meat fry a tiny portion in a pan and taste then re-season the raw mixture if necessary.

Cover the mince and chill in the refrigerator for at least 30 minutes, preferably a lot longer if possible to let it firm-up a bit.

Preheat a barbecue, tandoor or grill (broiler).

Take a 5 cm (2 in) ball of the mince in one hand and a skewer in the other (thick square metal ones are the best if you are not familiar with using rounded ones, or use soaked wooden ones).

Make the ball as smooth as possible by tossing it like a ball in your hand.

Now press the ball at roughly the middle of the skewer and press around so that the mince is now covering all round that part of the skewer.

Now apply a little oil or water to the palm that you use for the mince and gently press it into a sausage shape on the skewer. This does take a bit of practice and you may find that initially the mince falls off the skewer. Persevere! If you form a ring between your forefinger and thumb and use the rest of the fingers to guide the mince you will be fine. The pressure has to be gently applied and the mince pushed upwards so that it thins itself out over the skewer. Ideally the size of the sausage should be around 2.5 cm (1 in) or a bit less in diameter.

Once you have achieved this you can suspend the skewer on a small tray so that the skewer rests over the two opposite sides and allows the minced area to remain in the hollow of the tray. Repeat with the remaining meat and skewers.

Barbecue, grill (broil) or cook in a tandoor for 8–10 minutes, turning once until golden and cooked through but still moist and juicy inside (they should feel spongy if gently pressed).

Serve with green chutney and kachumber, or roll in chapattis or flour tortillas filled with salad and sliced onion.

100 g (3½ oz/scant ½ cup) chickpeas
    (garbanzos) or a 400 g (14 oz/1¾ cups)
    can, well drained

rock salt, to taste

2 large potatoes, scrubbed

100 g (3½ oz/ ½ cup) broken cashew
    nuts, or whole, broken or chopped
    into pieces

¼ tsp vegetable oil

1 large beef tomato

1 smallish red onion, finely chopped
    (optional)

1 heaped tbsp chopped coriander
    (cilantro) leaves

1–2 green chillies, finely chopped

1 tsp chaat masala powder, or to taste
    juice of ¼ lime (about 1 tsp)

ALOO CHANNA CAJU CHAAT

POTATO, CHICKPEA AND CASHEW SALAD

Serves 4–6

Chaat in many Indian languages simply means 'to lick'. This is easy to use as a term, as many of the little street-side snacks are eaten with the fingers and then you, naturally, gleefully lick them as the food itself is so tasty. Chaats, therefore, is a term for finger food, but also a name for the particular masala powder known as chaat masala used to flavour the snack or salad.

This is a cold salad, one of the many fruit- and vegetable-based ones that exist, and you can chop and change it as you like by experimenting with fresh ingredients that blend well with the masala. Chaats like this are often eaten in the afternoon, combined with fruits such as pineapple, banana, pomegranate or half-ripe mangoes as a summer cooler, the rock salt acting as a rehydrant to the body.

If using raw dried chickpeas, soak them overnight in cold water then boil in water until tender. Chickpeas will take from anywhere between 20 minutes to an hour to soften. They should not be firm as that can give you an upset tummy. Boiling chickpeas can take a long time even after soaking, as it is essential that they are thoroughly cooked. A pressure cooker is much faster. Add a little salt then drain thoroughly. Alternatively, drain the can of chickpeas in a colander, rinse with cold water and drain again.

Boil the potatoes in their skins until tender when pierced. Drain, and when cool enough to handle, peel then cut into 5 mm (¼ in) dice and put in a large bowl.

Preheat the oven to 120°C/250°F/gas ½. Mix the cashew nuts with the vegetable oil until they are all coated and spread out on a baking tray (please do not add more oil even if you think it is not enough, ¼ teaspoon is adequate). Gently roast in the oven until lightly coloured. Remove, leave to cool, then add to the potatoes.

Cut the tomato in quarters then remove the pulp with a teaspoon and reserve for use in a soup or sauce. Finely dice the flesh (you need about 3 heaped tablespoons). Add to the nuts and potato.

Add all the remaining ingredients, toss together gently, add salt to taste and more chilli, chaat masala or lime juice, if desired. Serve in a bowl to share, or plate individually and serve as a starter with hot pooris (see pages 180 and 189), as an accompaniment to another starter or as a side dish with a meal. Please note that this dish does not keep well in the refrigerator once it has all been mixed, so only combine at the very last minute, when ready to serve.

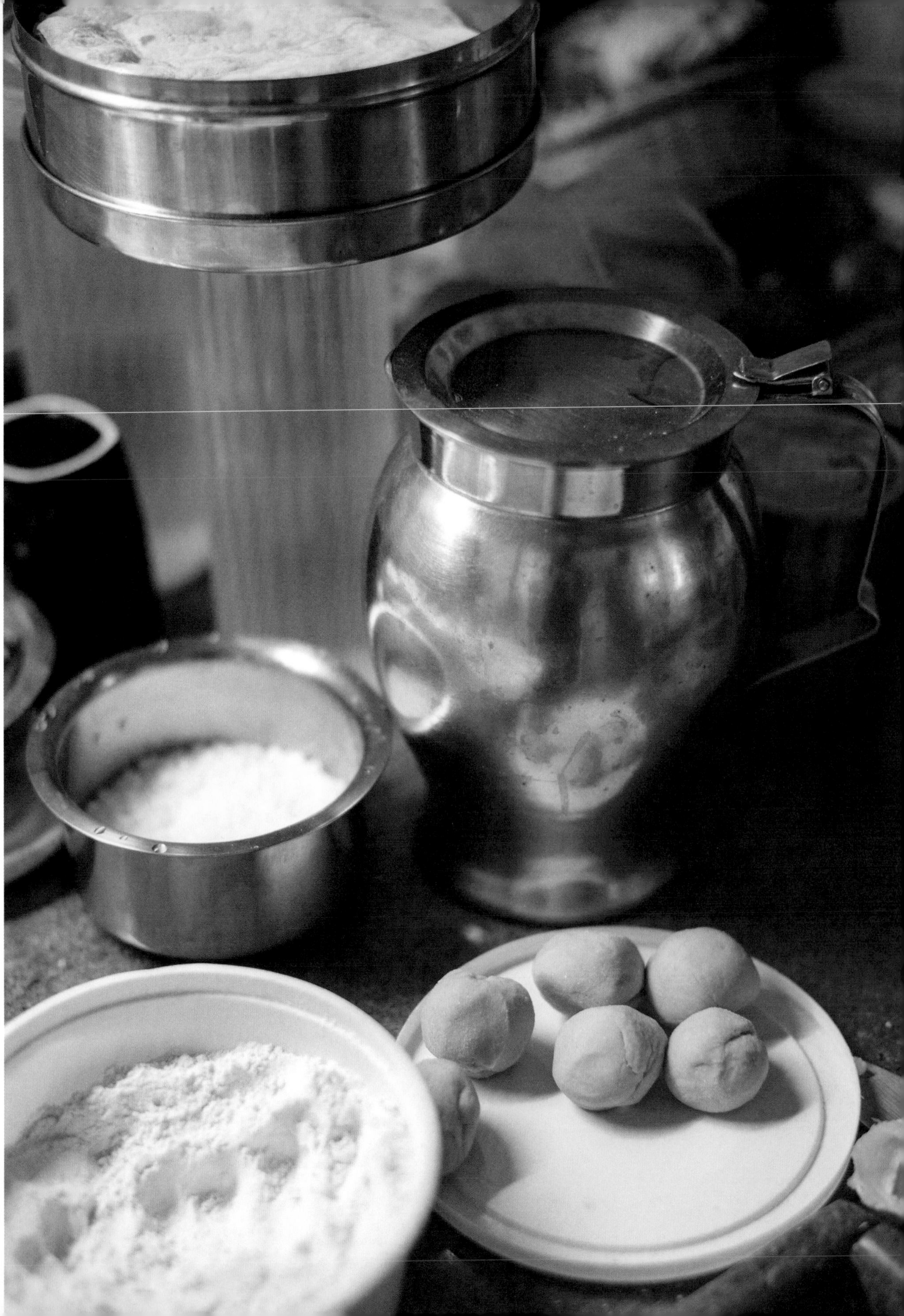

BREAD & RICE

There is not a single nation on the globe that does not have at its base some form of bread. In India we are a land of bread eaters (contrary to the belief that we might be just rice eaters). Across the country hundreds of types of flat breads exist, using every single grain grown in the subcontinent from gluten-free to wheat, chickpeas to rice, corn to millet – you name it and it's there – and these are eaten from breakfast to the end of the day. Just exploring the topic of Indian breads, might take me on a fifty-year-long journey across the subcontinent and even then I might not cover every ground.

Whenever I mention bread in the book, I do not mean sliced European bread unless, I have specified it. In India we have the most gorgeous breads. One of them happens to be the most common amongst all and is known as *ladi pao* meaning tray bread. This is similar to small cobs but contains no preservatives or bread improvers, which make modern bread unnatural and extra-light. *Pain rustique* or a baguette are the best alternatives.

In Bombay, bread – as in yeast-fermented dough bread – is most common. The Portuguese were the grand masters of bread-making and bread is one of the many things that helped their sailors survive the long journeys they made. While fermented dough was common along coastal regions using Toddy (where my name comes from as well as the English term for Hot Toddy) it is the Portuguese that first introduced hot baked bread to Bombay as a staple.

Bombay is famous for its breads of varying kinds, from sweet buns to little loaves, large loaves to sandwich loaves, flavoured loaves to amazingly crusty breads all prepared to satisfy the desires of a bread-hooked population. Nowhere else in India except for Goa, which is also Portuguese influenced of course, are the people so committed to enjoying their bread.

In my family it was like a religion and if, on any one day, the bread delivered was not perfectly baked, Mum would be most unhappy, and the bread man would get an earful, simply because her famous toasts would not come out perfect. Incidentally my mother's toasts became legendary and are nicknamed Granu Toasts by her grandchildren. My sister still makes them and we do too, but only from time to time as they are so time consuming when made to perfection. You need to buy good proper bread, not large, sticky cheap loaves.

Rice, on the other hand, is that grain which we all love and again have our favourite varieties. The world may not know that there exists nearly 100,000 different types of rice and the subcontinent itself grows roughly eighteen hundred of these or perhaps even more. That gives its people an amazing range and variety to choose from. For instance my parents favourite was Surti Kolum or 'silky rice' from Surat and later, when in Poona, I was introduced to Aamba Mohur or 'mango blossom' and it did have the aroma of mango blossom. Instantly, Pervin and I fell in love with it and to this day we bring some back with us each year and share it with no one! We eat it with my all-time favourite *dhaan daar* or rice with simple Parsee-style lentils.

Rice is a staple for many people in India, but in the Punjab, where the king of all rice – basmati – grows, it is not. Basmati is a revered rice and not one to be used on a day-to-day basis. Good basmati is reserved for special occasions and a good well-aged bag of basmati, five to six years old or older, would fetch the same value as a well-aged Burgundy.

MASALA POORI

POORIS WITH SPICES

Makes 15–20 depending on size

A masala as we all know by now is a combination of spices and condiments and naturally an item with the word masala attached to it is open to variations. This is a typical recipe for crispy-spiced pooris, but you can experiment and try it out with different flavoured spicing.

A poori, poorie or puri is a fried chapatti of sorts. Poori comes in various shapes and sizes but they are always fried. They can be soft or crisp – it all depends on the recipe and what you wish to serve them with. It can be a snack or it can be part of a main meal. Also, pooris are a matter of trial and error so do not give up simply because you did not get them right the first time. I can assure you that I am no champion myself, and my wife can make them better by a mile than me any day. It's all a matter of practice and the first few will not always look good or even shapely for that matter but they'll still taste good!

Sift the flour with the salt in a large stainless steel bowl or the bowl of a food processor.

Add all the other ingredients except the butter, ghee or oil and water, then rub in the fat.

Gradually add water a little at a time, kneading by hand or in the machine to form a firm dough. You may need more or less water depending on the flour. It is important that it is not sticky at all.

Wrap in clingfilm (plastic wrap) or a damp cloth and leave to rest for around 15–20 minutes.

Heat 5–7.5 cm (2–3 in) oil for deep-frying. At the same time get ready a sieve (strainer), some kitchen towel spread on a tray and a slotted or holed frying spoon.

Roll out the dough as thinly as possible, on a lightly floured surface if absolutely necessary. Cut out 5–7.5 cm (2–3 in) discs of dough (brush off any excess flour if any was used for rolling).

To test if the oil is hot enough, drop in one poori. It should rise to the surface immediately and cook quickly to golden brown. Fry no more than 2 or 3 discs at a time. The best technique is to hold them down whilst spinning each one in the hot oil for a few seconds and then release them, flip them over as soon as they bloat and colour lightly. Remove quickly as they will cook in seconds.

Drain on paper towels and serve hot. Enjoy with sweet chutney or potato bhajee. They make a suberb dessert if served with crushed cardamom-flavoured mango pulp.

400 g (14 oz/3½ cups) wholemeal flour
1 level tsp salt
2 heaped tbsp chopped coriander
(cilantro) leaves and stalks
2 green chillies, finely minced
1 tsp ground anardana
(pomegranate seeds), (optional)
½ tsp coarsely crushed black
peppercorns
½ tsp chilli powder
½ tsp cumin seeds, roasted and crushed
1 tbsp melted butter, ghee or oil
approximately 200 ml
(7 fl oz/ scant 1 cup) water
sunflower or rapeseed oil for
deep-frying

To serve
sweet chutney or potato bhajee

450 g (1 lb/3 cups) medium cornmeal

1½ tsp salt

about 200 ml (7 fl oz/scant 1 cup)
   cold water

2 heaped tbsp melted ghee or butter
   (though butter can burn)

MAKKI KI ROTI

CORNMEAL CHAPATTIS

Makes 6–8

Whereas certain regions of India like The Punjab and parts of Rajasthan have a particular culture for eating *Makki ki Roti*, other regions of India will prepare them from time to time. This bread is also synonymous with the harvest festival of Punjab. Indians have been making cornmeal rotis for centuries, however it is the advent of the Mexican corn tortilla which has made cornmeal bread so popular and it is often difficult to explain to people that Indians too have been making cornmeal breads for hundreds of years. They are easy to make but care must be taken when rolling out the dough balls. Since corn has no gluten, the dough dries out quickly and breaks up so they are best made one at a time. Don't be put off, though, it does not take as long as you may imagine to make. They are best eaten warm with spinach or mustard greens known as *sarson ka saag*.

Sift the flour and salt together using a medium-holed sieve (strainer), or simply mix them together.

Divide into more or less equal portions on the work surface and take one small mound at a time.

Mix and knead with the fingers to form a stiff dough by adding only very little water at a time.

Grease the griddle well with ghee or butter over a low heat and place the dough ball in the middle.

With the flat of your palm, flatten the dough ball by pressing down in the middle and outwards until you have a thin pancake-sized chapatti. Remember that the griddle is hot so keep your palm well opened and fingers away from the pan edge. Once flattened flip it over gently and then cook until you have the desired colour on both sides.

Repeat with each mound of flour, adding a little more ghee or butter to the griddle before cooking each one. Keep them warm, wrapped in a clean cloth or napkin, whilst cooking the remainder. Serve warm.

250 g (9 oz/2¼ cups) wholemeal flour,
    plus extra for dusting

1 tsp salt

1 tbsp sunflower or rapeseed oil, warmed

cold water to mix

a little melted ghee or butter
    (or use more oil)

CHAPATTIS

WHOLEMEAL FLATBREADS

Makes 6–8

It is very difficult to give an absolute recipe for
chapattis. It is merely a matter of experience
and how well you understand the dough you are
preparing. Persevere. Here is a basic one to work
with. But remember all flour differs in how it
behaves. Keep experimenting and you'll eventually
get a 'feel' for it and know when the dough is right.
In hotels and restaurants throughout India where
you see chapattis on the menu, there is always a
specialist employed to make them!

Mix the flour and salt together in a bowl and stir in the warm oil. Add water a
tablespoon at a time and knead into a firm smooth ball.

Knead well for a few minutes until the dough does not stick and feels firm to
the touch but not hard. Cover with another bowl or clingfilm (plastic wrap), and
set aside for an hour or two.

Re-knead then form into a smooth ball and dust with flour.

Divide into 2.5 cm (1 in) balls.

Brush a griddle pan or tava with a little melted ghee, butter, or oil and place over
a medium heat. You do not want it smoking hot or the chapatti will brown instantly
and not cook through.

Place each ball on a floured surface and flatten with your palm or fingers, then
roll out as thin as possible into rounds (do remember that even the big chefs and
people such as myself with twenty years of experience cannot always roll out
smooth, round chapattis as well as our mothers or wives can – this will give you
some confidence when you end up plotting the world in different shapes!).

Dust off any excess flour on the chapatti and place it flat on the griddle or tava.
Flip it over after about 30 seconds, brush with melted fat or oil on one side and
flip over again. A good chapatti is one which does not show burn marks but cooks
through and is lightly browned.

When done, fold over into half and place on a clean cloth or paper towels in a
container with a lid.

Serve the warm chapattis with most savoury dishes as an accompaniment.

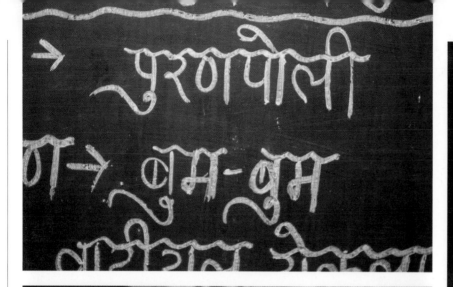

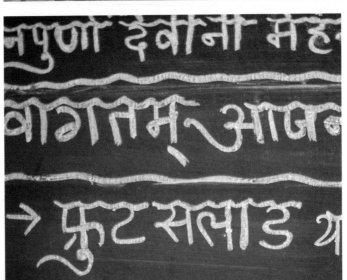

400 g (14 oz/3½ cups) plain
(all-purpose) flour
½ – ¾ tsp salt
¾ tsp baking powder
1 heaped tsp caster (superfine) sugar
1 egg
100 ml (3½ fl oz/scant ½ cup)
plain yoghurt
1–2 tbsp hot milk
a little butter or ghee
a few tbsp hot water
vegetable oil for deep-frying

BHATURA

PUFFED WHITE POORI

Makes 6–8

These puffy deep-fried breads are larger in size and heavier than the flatbreads. They are traditionally eaten as an accompaniment to channa masala or *aloo ki subzi*. Allow one or two per person with kachumber (see page 93) and some thick plain yoghurt. The recipe given here is very workable indeed and don't fret if you do not always succeed. *Bhaturas* are temperamental and will give you intermittent pleasures of getting the perfect one, well puffed and golden brown. However even the flat ones will taste good! We have made them smaller which makes it easier to fry. The only drawback is that you will have to give yourself time to make them so prepare the dough in the morning and cook them in the evening.

Sift the flour, salt, baking powder and sugar together.

Beat the egg into the yoghurt in a bowl, add the hot milk and 2 tablespoons of hot water.

Gradually mix the yoghurt mixture into the flour and start kneading. If the dough is too dry add a little more water but only a tablespoon at a time. Knead well to form a soft, smooth elastic dough.

Grease your palms with a little butter or ghee and knead the dough to form a large round ball.

Place the ball in a bowl, cover with a damp cloth and set aside at room temperature for 6–8 hours to prove.

Get everything in place ready to cook the breads. Pour enough oil for deep-frying in a wok or kadhai, a slotted spoon and colander placed over a bowl for removing the bhaturas and draining them, flour for dusting, a rolling pin and, of course, the food with which they are to be served.

Remove the dough from the bowl and re-knead it gently.

Divide the dough into 6–8 equal balls. The size is a matter for you but they need to be able to fit nicely into the oil for frying and small ones are probably preferable to very large. Handle as little as possible.

Heat the oil for deep-frying to almost smoking point.

Meanwhile, roll out each ball, using as little flour as necessary to prevent sticking, to about 3 mm (⅛ in) thick. Fry one at a time in the hot oil until golden brown and puffed. Flip them over lightly, if necessary, to brown evenly all over. (One way that works is to push the bhatura with your frying spoon and spin it at the same time. This motion of them spinning in the hot oil will make then puff up quicker and look nicer. If, however, the rolling out is not even you will have thick edges and a very thin centre and no ballooning. Practice makes perfect!)

BHAKHRI

GRIDDLED MASALA ROTI

Makes 10–12

Bhakhri is made in several different ways. One is the Gujarati way in which spices are not added. The Maharashtrian way includes the addition of certain spices and condiments. This is a simple, slightly modified recipe and is one of those breads that you can store in a heap, or even have it a couple of days later by re-griddling to a crisp texture. *Bhakhri* can be stuffed as in a *paratha*, which is a bit tedious or, like here, simply rolled out into discs and griddled with a little extra fat when being cooked.

Sift the flour with the turmeric, chilli powder, salt and the asafoetida, if using. Rub in 3 tablespoons of the oil, melted butter or ghee and stir in the cumin. Add the yoghurt and mix it in well.

Knead to form a smooth, firm dough. If the dough is too hard and does not come together, add a little more yoghurt to achieve the right consistency. Wrap in clingfilm (plastic wrap) or a damp cloth and leave to rest for at least an hour.

Re-knead and roll out into a long sausage with your hands. Divide into 10 or 12 equal portions.

Preheat a griddle pan or tava. Form each portion into a ball then flatten and roll out into thin discs. Brush with a little oil, melted butter or ghee to get a crisp texture and even colouring. Fry until lightly browned underneath, flip over, brush with a little more fat and cook the other side. Flip over one more time then remove from the pan and place on a plate covered with a clean cloth or kitchen towel. Cover and keep warm while cooking the remainder.

They are fantastic eaten with thick yoghurt and some mango or any other type of chutney.

500 g (1 lb 2 oz/4 ½ cups)
wholemeal flour

½ tsp ground turmeric

1 tsp chilli powder

1½ tsp salt

pinch of ground asafoetida (optional)

6 tbsp oil, melted butter, or ghee

1 tsp cumin seeds, toasted
and roughly ground

120 ml (4 fl oz/ ½ cup) live
plain yoghurt

To serve

thick plain yoghurt and mango or
other chutney (see pages 212–219)

MISSIE ROTI

FLATTENED BREAD WITH CHICKPEA FLOUR AND SPINACH

Makes 12

Different parts of the subcontinent use different flours for flatbreads, depending on the staple grain of that region. Some choose corn, others wholemeal flour or just white flour. This combines three, including delicious, nutty chickpea flour as I like it that way. However, you can use just one or two of them if that is all that is available. Simply increase the amounts accordingly. This one is a particularly popular delight. In fact, it's often our dinner when we are tired and all we have is some stale roti in the fridge along with yoghurt and chutney!

Sift all 3 flours and the salt together in a large bowl or a food processor.

Either finely chop the spinach and the red onion and add it to the flour or, alternatively, give them a few rounds in the food processor until they are finely chopped, then add the flour. Add the warm oil and mix with enough water to form a firm dough (remember that all flours vary and some absorb more water than others). Knead by hand for several minutes or run the machine for 1 minute until the dough is smooth and elastic.

Shape the dough into a large ball and leave covered with clingfilm (plastic wrap) or a damp cloth for at least 30 minutes to rest.

It may happen the resting time this will soften the dough and this is fine, but if it gets too soft you may need to add some chickpea flour to make it dry again.

To make the roti, divide the dough into 12 even-sized balls on a floured surface. Pat a ball of dough out thinly to about 3 mm (⅛ in) thick. It need not be round: oval is just as good. Brush with a little oil or melted butter and sprinkle with a little flour.

Fold the two edges over to the middle, apply some more melted butter and flour and fold over again to form a layered strip. Stretch it a bit and then, holding it between the thumb and forefinger of one hand, and with the thumb and forefinger of the other hand, gradually start to coil it up like a flat pinwheel. Repeat with all the dough balls.

Place a griddle pan or tava over a medium heat. Roll out a roti coil, on a lightly floured surface if necessary, as thinly as possible – no more than 1–3 mm (¹⁄₁₀ to ⅛ in) thick. Dust off any excess flour before placing it on the pan. Cook until light brown on the underside. Whilst this is happening you can begin to roll the next one.

Flip the browned roti over and brush with a little melted butter. Once the other side is browned flip over and apply some butter on this side too. Now flip over once or twice and remove onto a plate lined with a clean kitchen cloth or paper towels. Cover and keep warm while cooking the remainder.

Wipe the surface of the pan with paper towels before putting the next roti on. When all the roti are cooked, serve straight away or they will keep well and can be reheated later in a warm oven or very briefly in the microwave. They are also good cold with a sweet chutney or pickle and plain, thick yoghurt.

250 g (9 oz/2¼ cups) chickpea
(garbanzo) or besan flour, plus extra for
dusting
150 g (5 oz/1¼ cups)
wholemeal flour
100 g (3½ oz/scant 1 cup) plain
(all-purpose) flour
1½ tsp salt
40–50 baby spinach leaves
1 red onion
about 200 ml (7 fl oz/scant 1 cup) water
1½ tbsp sunflower or
rapeseed oil, warmed
2 tbsp melted butter

500 g (1 lb 2 oz/2½ cups) basmati rice

3–4 litres (102–136 fl oz/

   12¾–16 cups) water

1–2 tbsp sunflower or rapeseed oil

   or a good knob of butter

1–2 tsp salt or to taste

5 cm (2 in) piece of cinnamon stick

6 green cardamom pods, split

1–2 bay leaves

1 blade of mace

1 tsp cumin seeds, toasted

BAAFAELA CHAWAL

BOILED RICE

Makes 4–6 portions

Baafaela Chawal is Gujarati for boiled rice, it's
oobla hua chawal in Hindi. It doesn't have to be
just plain cooked, though: we often add fragrant
flavourings as in this recipe but you can omit them
if you prefer. There are several different ways to
cook rice – it can be steamed or cooked by the
absorption method but here we've used the draining
method which produces lovely fluffy grains.

Wash the rice gently, drain and set aside for 15–30 minutes.

Bring the water to the boil in a large saucepan with the oil or butter and the salt.

Add the rice and all the flavourings and stir slowly for the first 2–3 minutes
to separate all the grains. Some rice takes as little as 6–8 minutes to cook, others
about 10, so check the packet directions. Test frequently. The rice should be tender
but still with some 'bite'.

Drain in a colander over a bowl, reserving the cooking liquid. Fluff up the
rice with a fork to separate the grains. Leave the spices in the rice or remove, if
preferred.

The reserved liquid can be used for cooking. In my house it gets converted into
nice soups for the family, either with diced vegetables and herbs and some meat if
you like, or it is converted into a creamed soup where a mixture of vegetables are
simmered in it then the whole lot puréed.

115 g (4 oz/½ cup) dried chickpeas
(garbanzos), soaked in cold water
overnight or a 425 g (15½ oz/ 2 cups)
can, drained

5 tbsp sunflower or rapeseed oil

5 cm (2 in) piece of cinnamon stick
or cassia bark

3–4 cloves

1–2 whole red chillies, broken in half

5–6 garlic cloves, finely chopped

4 onions, halved and thinly sliced

400–500 g (14 oz–1 lb 2 oz/2–2¼ cups)
basmati rice

about 2 tsp salt, or to taste

about 750 ml (25 fl oz/3 cups) boiling water
or stock (1½ times the volume of rice)

2 tbsp chopped coriander (cilantro) leaves

CHOLEY PALAV

CHICKPEA PULAO

Makes 4–6 portions

Chickpeas (garbanzos) come in many different varieties. The most popular of them all is the large white variety, known as Bengali Channa. High in protein, chickpeas can be used in several different ways. This is a simple pulao and makes an excellent accompaniment to many of India's great dishes. If you can get Indian cassia bark, it imparts a better flavour than the usual cinnamon stick!

If using raw, soaked chickpeas, bring a pan of water to the boil, add the chickpeas and boil rapidly for 10 minutes to remove any toxins. Reduce the heat to medium and allow to simmer for about 45 minutes–1 hour or until tender. Season with a little salt then drain and set aside.

Heat 3 tablespoons of the oil in a deep pot or saucepan, which has a tight fitting lid. When the oil forms a haze but before it is smoking, add the cinnamon stick, cloves and chillies. Stir and as soon as you see the cloves swell, add the cumin and sauté for a minute or so.

Add the garlic and, 30 seconds later, half the sliced onions. Sauté until the garlic is just beginning to colour.

Now reduce the heat, add the rice and salt and stir for a minute or two, turning well and levelling out each time so that the rice gets an all round heat.

Add water to come about 2 cm (¾ in) above the level of the rice (or use the measured amount, but this is simpler and works very well).

Stir for a few seconds and allow to rest, covered.

Reduce the heat as low as possible.

Stir again every minute or so until most of the water is absorbed but you can just detect water around the sides.

Add the boiled or canned and drained chickpeas. Stir, cover the pot but ensure that all the sides are clean of grains when you are about to cover.

Check every one or two minutes, give the rice a gentle stir from the bottom up but very gently until hot through, the rest of the water is absorbed and the chickpeas are hot through. It should take 30–40 minutes to cook.

Check your seasoning and whether or not the rice is cooked.

Meanwhile, heat the remaining oil in a frying pan. Add the remaining onions and fry over a medium heat for about 6 minutes until a rich, golden brown, stirring frequently.

Serve the pulao topped with the browned onions and sprinkled with the chopped coriander.

This rice can also be cooked in the oven. When it has nearly absorbed the water, cover, and put in the overn at 130°C/266°F/ ½ gas for 15 minutes. Stir with a fork and serve piping hot.

2–3 heaped tbsp raw peanuts

5–6 black peppercorns

1–2.5 cm (½–1 in) piece of cinnamon stick

3–4 cloves

1 tsp coriander seeds

1 heaped tsp sesame seeds

2–3 heaped tbsp desiccated
(shredded) coconut

1 heaped tsp cumin seeds

8–10 tendlis (fresh gherkins),
or 1 large courgette (zucchini)

60–75 ml (2–2½ fl oz/¼ – ⅓ cup
sunflower oil or ghee

½ tsp black mustard seeds

good pinch of ground asafoetida

10–12 curry leaves (preferably fresh)

2 waxy potatoes, peeled and cubed

1 aubergine (eggplant), cubed

4–5 heaped tbsp (about 125 g/4½ oz/
generous cup) shelled fresh
or frozen peas

3–4 green chillies, chopped

250–300 g (9–10½ oz/
1¼ –1½ cups) basmati rice, rinsed
and soaked

½ tsp ground turmeric

1 heaped tbsp raw cashew nuts,
roughly chopped

salt to taste

handful of coriander (cilantro)
leaves, chopped

1–2 heaped tbsp butter or ghee

To garnish

freshly grated coconut (optional)

MASALA BHAAT

SPICED VEGETABLE RICE

Serves 4

I simply couldn't write this chapter without
including this great Maharashtrian speciality.
I grew up eating several versions in several different
homes: each friend's mother claimed to have the
best recipe handed down from her grandmother.
How could I not say to them all that each one's was
the best when I was getting a feast and all of them
were truly spectacular? I am hoping to come a close
second with my recipe as I am using all the hints
I picked up from some great masters. Naturally,
no matter how hard chefs like me try, we can never
match a mother's touch.

Masala Bhaat is a type of vegetable pulao with
a combination of spices and nuts to make it an
interesting and flavoursome dish. It is best eaten
with a thin daal and, of course, a good pickle or
chutney. The preparation may look extensive and
the list of ingredients certainly does, but, believe
me, it is worth a try.

If the peanuts are not skinned soak them in water for 15–20 minutes, drain and rub
off the skins in a clean cloth.

In a wok or frying pan, dry roast the peppercorns, cinnamon, cloves, coriander
seeds, sesame seeds, coconut and half the cumin seeds over a low heat until
fragrant and the coconut is pale golden. Alternatively preheat the oven to
160°C/325°F/gas 3 and roast them spread out on a baking tray for 4–5 minutes,
switch off the oven and leave them in there for 30 minutes. Grind to a powder in a
clean coffee grinder or small food processor, in a mortar with a pestle or in a small
bowl with the end of a rolling pin. Set aside.

If you can get the tendlis (or tindoras as they are also known) wash them, snip off
the two tips and then cut lengthways into four. If using a courgette cut in quarters
widthways, then cut in batons.

In a flameproof casserole add the oil or ghee and heat to a slight haze.
Add the mustard seeds and, as soon as they crackle, add the remaining cumin seeds
and asafoetida.

As soon as the crackling stops, add the curry leaves and all the vegetables,
including the green chillies.

Sauté for 5–6 minutes and then add the rice and the turmeric. Mix well.

Sauté for 3–5 minutes and add the ground spices, the cashew nuts and the peanuts.

Spread everything out evenly in the pot and add enough water to cover the
rice by 2.5 cm (1 in). Add salt now and taste the liquid.

Bring to the boil, reduce heat to low, cover the pot tightly and cook until the rice
is fully cooked and dry, about 20 minutes.

Remove the lid and let it stand for a minute or two to dry. Add the butter or
ghee on top, and the chopped coriander and mix gently but well. If you have any
fresh coconut, grate it and sprinkle it on the top before serving.

LAAPSI KHICHDI A'LA PERVIN

WET RICE AND LENTILS WITH ONION AND TOMATO

Serves 4

This is a great Khichdi and one that has become a favourite in our family. However, my wife has perfected her own recipe by trial and error based on the tastes, likes and dislikes of us all, so I cannot claim mine is, necessarily, the best! Flavourings vary from household to household but onion, garlic and tomato are common to all. Laapsi is another word for 'wet' but the result is more moist and slightly glutinous from the starch in the rice rather than swilling in liquid, which the name implies.

This is traditionally served with *choonda* (a typical Gujarati-style chutney made by mixing spices and sugar with shredded or grated raw mango and leaving it in the sun to mature). Use yellow lentils or split peas if you can't get the split mung beans.

Wash the rice and lentils well together then cover with cold water and leave to soak while preparing the vegetables.

Heat the oil in a large casserole with a tight-fitting lid. Sauté the cumin seeds for about 30 seconds until fragrant then add the asafoetida and the garlic. Keep stirring to prevent the spices from burning.

As soon as the garlic changes colour add the chopped onions and sauté until the onions are soft and lightly golden, about 5 minutes.

Drain the rice and lentils and add to the casserole with the tomatoes, turmeric, chilli powder and ground cumin. Stir for a minute or two then add the water.

Add the butter and salt, cover and cook over a medium heat for 30–40 minutes, stirring from time to time to prevent sticking. Unlike most rice dishes, the rice needs to be well-cooked so do not worry if it gets mushy, that's what Laapsi should be. If it's drying out, add a little more water to keep it really moist.

As soon as the rice and the daal are cooked and the Khichdi has the consistency of porridge, remove from the heat and stir in the coriander.

Serve with *choonda* or mango chutney, papadums and shredded spring onions.

400 g (14 oz/2 cups) basmati rice

200 g (7 oz/ generous 1 cup) split yellow mung beans (moong daal)

1 red onion, finely chopped

4 garlic cloves, crushed or finely chopped

2–3 tomatoes, roughly chopped

2 tbsp sunflower or rapeseed oil

1 tsp cumin seeds

generous pinch of ground asafoetida

½ tsp ground turmeric

¼ tsp chilli powder

¼ tsp ground cumin

1.2 litres (40 fl oz/5 cups) water

1 heaped tbsp butter

1 tsp salt

1 heaped tbsp chopped coriander (cilantro) leaves

To serve

choonda or hot and sweet mango chutney, papadums and shredded spring onions (scallions)

500 g (1 lb 2 oz) lean lamb, diced

200 ml (7 fl oz/scant 1 cup) plain
Greek-style yoghurt

vegetable or rapeseed oil for deep-frying

500 g (1 lb 2 oz) onions, halved and
very thinly sliced

For the masala

500 g (1 lb 2 oz) onions, thinly sliced

100 ml (3½ fl oz/scant ½ cup) oil
reserved from earlier
onion deep-frying

2 cm (¾ in) piece of cinnamon stick

4–5 green cardamom pods, split

3–4 cloves

2–3 large red chillies, left whole

2 large green chillies, finely chopped

5 cm (2 in) piece fresh ginger,
finely chopped

4–6 garlic cloves

1 tsp ground cumin

2 tsp ground coriander

1 tsp chilli powder

½ tsp ground turmeric

300–400 ml (10–14 fl oz/
1¼ –1¾ cups) water

salt to taste

For the pulao

500 g (1 lb 2 oz/2½ cups) basmati rice

4–5 litres (136–170 fl oz/
16–20¼ cups) water

2 bay leaves

4–5 green cardamom pods, split

1 tsp salt

CYRUSÍ GOS NO PULAO

CYRUS'S LAMB PULAO

Serves 4

There are many recipes for Lamb Pulao (or pilaf) with each person claiming that his or hers is the very best. This is a time-tested one by me: I have tweaked and added to some old recipes and traditions and come up with a recipe which is more foolproof than many I have tried. Pulaos are indulgent food, always eaten at celebrations and festive occasions or when you just want to treat yourself. Remember that in the subcontinent top-quality basmati is used for pulaos and biryanis. Basmati is graded by age and quality. Most households will store good rice in airtight containers and use it in rotation but never in the year it was produced. Older rice has a better aroma and, if kept well, ages like a good wine!

Mix the lamb with the yoghurt in a container with a lid. Cover and leave in the refrigerator overnight.

The next day, heat oil for deep-frying and fry the onions until crisp and golden. Remove with a slotted spoon, drain in a colander over a bowl and set aside. Reserve the oil. When the onions have drained, tip them into a separate container so the colander and bowl are ready for the masala onions.

To prepare the masala, wash the onions well in cold water and drain thoroughly. Remove as much water as you can before frying (if you have a salad spinner, use that. Alternatively, wrap in paper towels and pat well).

Heat the oil and fry the onion, stirring regularly until lightly golden, then transfer with a slotted spoon to the colander over a bowl to drain. They will continue cooking in the latent heat and be deep golden when cooled.

Add the whole spices to the onion oil. Stir until they sizzle, swell and brown but do not allow them to burn. Immediately add the sliced browned onions and sauté a few minutes until richly coloured. Remove the fried onion and masala with a slotted spoon, squeezing as much oil back into the pan as possible.

Reheat the oil to smoking point and add the marinated meat. Do not stir much, allow it to sear on all sides. Once brown continue to sauté until almost dry. Add the chopped green chilli, ginger and garlic and sauté until the garlic begins to lightly colour.

Blend the ground spices in the water and add to the lamb with a little salt. Bring to the boil, reduce the heat and simmer until most of the liquid has evaporated and the mixture is almost dry again, stirring occasionally so the mixture does not stick. Stir in the sautéed brown onions and whole spices, and add a little more water, if necessary, to moisten. Cover tightly with a lid and cook over a low heat for about 40 minutes until the lamb is almost tender and bathed in a rich sauce (the lamb won't be completely tender, it will finish cooking in the oven). Taste and re-season if necessary.

Meanwhile prepare the pulao. Bring the water to the boil in a large saucepan with the bay leaves, cardamom and salt.

Wash the rice well in a bowl until the water runs clear, drain and set aside.

Continued overleaf

CYRUSÍ GOS NO PULAO
CYRUS'S LAMB PULAO

Continued from previous page

When the water is boiling rapidly, add the rice and stir continuously for a minute or two over a high heat. Boil for 6–7 minutes or until the grains are almost tender (it is best to keep the rice just slightly underdone as it will be baked later). Drain in a colander, discard the flavourings, if preferred, and set aside.

To finish the pulao, preheat the oven to 150°C/302°F/gas 2. In a small saucepan or frying pan gently heat the saffron until it becomes crisp and fragrant. Do not allow the saffron to burn or singe. At no stage should you leave it unattended! Immediately add the water and slowly heat to a simmer then cover and set aside to infuse.

Put half the boiled rice in a bowl and mix in the saffron water. Get every saffron strand out of the pan (add a few more grains of the rice to the pan and stir round to absorb any residue, then tip into the bowl).

Pour the melted butter into a large casserole or saucepan with a tight-fittin lid that will take all the rice and meat, and make sure it coats the base. Mix about half of the reserved fried onions into the remaining cooked rice, and add it to the casserole, levelling the top. Sprinkle over half the coriander and mint, and arrange half the tomatoes and potatoes over the top.

Gently spread all the lamb on top, including all its sauce and scrape the pan clean with a spatula. Scatter the remaining coriander, mint, tomatoes and potatoes on top. Cut the eggs into halves and place them, yolk side up, evenly in between the potato and tomato pieces. Now cover evenly with the saffron rice. Sprinkle the remaining fried onions (retain a spoonful to use as a garnish later) and the lime juice over the rice.

Cover tightly with the lid. If the lid is not tight-fitting, place a sheet of foil over the casserole before putting on the lid. In India we would seal the pot with dough to make a perfect seal. You can do that instead. It does not damage the pot and will break off once fully baked. Simply mix flour and water to a pliable dough and press it all round the edge sealing the lid to the rim of the pot.

Bake in the centre of the oven for 1½ hours. After about 40 minutes reduce the temperature to 120°C/250°F/gas ½. Do not be tempted to take the lid off and look – the steam must be kept inside the pot.

When you are ready to serve open the pot and gently mix the layers together. Remove into large platters and serve garnished with the reserved browned onions, if liked, with masala daal, cucumber raita and kachumber.

To finish

a good pinch of saffron strands

150 ml (5 fl oz/²⁄₃ cup) cold water

2 tbsp melted butter

2–3 heaped tbsp chopped coriander
(cilantro) leaves

2 heaped tbsp chopped mint leaves

2–3 tomatoes, quartered

3–4 boiled potatoes, peeled and cubed

3–4 hard-boiled eggs, shelled

juice of 1 lime

To serve

masala daal or some simple
cucumber raita and some fresh
kachumber (see page 93)

800 g–1 kg tomatoes,
halved or quartered

about 1 litre (34 fl oz/4¼ cups)
boiling water

2.5 cm (1 in) piece of fresh ginger

4–6 garlic cloves

3 tbsp sunflower or rapeseed oil

2 white or red onions, halved
and thinly sliced

400–500 g (14 oz–1 lb 2 oz/
2–2½ cups) basmati rice

5–6 black peppercorns

2–3 cloves

2 heaped tbsp chopped coriander
(cilantro) leaves

salt to taste

To serve

thick, plain yoghurt to serve (optional)

TAMATAR KA BHAAT

TOMATO RICE

Serves 4

This simple yet flavourful recipe for Tomato Rice
is simply great and works very well. Also known as
tambatar cha bhaat it is yet another delicious way
to cook rice. It is an interesting addition to a meal
and can be accompanied by a great many meats,
vegetables and/or daals. I have chosen this version
to simply showcase the diversity of Indian cooking.
It is as modern as it is ancient.

Put the tomatoes in a large saucepan or casserole and add about 400–500 ml
(14–17 fl oz/1¾–2¼ cups) of the boiling water. Bring to the boil and boil for
8–10 minutes. Remove from the heat.

Meanwhile in a mortar and pestle (or a small bowl with the end of a rolling pin)
make a paste of the ginger and garlic. Add to the tomatoes and purée with a hand
blender or pass through a sieve (strainer).

Heat the oil in a frying pan, kadhai or wok and gently brown the sliced onions
for 5–10 minutes until golden.

Meanwhile wash and drain the rice thoroughly in a colander.

Add the peppercorns, cloves and rice to the onions and sauté for 2–3 minutes.

Add all of this to the puréed tomato mixture and return to the heat.

Add the remaining boiling water and some salt. Stir well, part-cover and bring
back to the boil. Stir well to ensure nothing is stuck to the bottom and scrape the
edges with a spatula to clean the sides so all the rice is in the pan. Cover tightly and
reduce the heat as low as possible. Simmer for 15–20 minutes until the rice is just
tender and has absorbed all the liquid. Stir once halfway through cooking but don't
keep lifting the lid.

Taste and re-season, if necessary. Serve with the coriander either stirred
through the rice or sprinkled on top. The tomato rice also tastes good served cold
with yoghurt.

PICKLES & CHUTNEYS

Whilst the internationally-accepted word chutney is Indian, the word pickle is truly British and today, as the British public is truly in love with Indian food, preserves and condiments we can truly say that everyone seems to be in a chutney situation!

The palate in Britain has changed so much in the past few years since we came to Britain (in late 1991) that I think today we probably have the most distinguished and discerning palate in the world!

The art of preservation is international and timeless and has been in practice ever since man started to understand the seasons. Every cuisine differs, depending on the region where it is evolved – the local surroundings, the produce, the meats, seafood and, most importantly, the climate. Unique preservation techniques are employed in the East where the climate is mostly tropical. Though adequate sunlight is available there are enough germs and bacterial warfare floating in the atmosphere to putrefy food very quickly so, to avoid that, spicing and oil become the key elements here, with spicing and sugar, for many chutneys.

In India chutneys and pickles are eaten with the meal and not as a little *amuse bouche* with papadums, mint sauce and neither also the traditional smashing of the papads as is British custom. If papads are eaten with drinks these are mostly always roasted but do not come with pickles and chutneys. That somehow is purely a British thing and I have never understood where it came from.

For the poor who cannot afford more than a thick, heavily made bread, more often than not a small piece of pickle or chutney is the only thing that gives them the benefit of taste and flavour and they eat that little spoonful with much relish. We use pickles and chutneys in India as condiments as well as partners to bread. These condiments are created to enhance the flavour of the food and bring non-seasonal products to the table.

In our restaurants we have never bought any ready-made chutneys or pickles since maybe 1995. Once we began making them all ourselves we only used ours and gradually got rid of the shop-bought mango chutney, which were buying buy due to demands from guests until that time. Guests now buy our chutneys instead!

Explore here the many ways in which you can extend the flavour of your condiments, and stretch your imagination a bit by making meals with them, glazes for roasts, blending them with pasta for an extra edge and so on.

NARIAL NI LEELI CHUTNEY

GREEN COCONUT CHUTNEY PARSEE STYLE

Makes 1 medium jar

This is a delicious variation of the Fresh Green Chutney on page 215. We Parsees prefer it to be rather minty and a bit on the hot and sour side but reduce the mint and chillies if preferred. It makes a great sandwich when spread over sliced boiled potato and tomato and wrapped in a chapatti or naan bread. We also eat this chutney with lentils and rice as an accompaniment.

If using desiccated coconut, mix it with 150 ml (5 fl oz/²⁄₃ cup) hot water and leave to soak for 1 hour until soft and rehydrated and the liquid is absorbed. If necessary, add up to 50 ml (2 fl oz/¼ cup) water during soaking.

Tip the coconut into a food processor and add all the remaining ingredients. Purée to a smooth paste, adding a splash of water if absolutely necessary.

Put in a streilized, screw-topped jar and store in the refrigerator. Use a dry spoon to remove the chutney and always clean the sides before re-sealing to preserve the freshness. Best eaten within 2 weeks.

1 coconut, grated or 200 g (7 oz/
2¼ cups) desiccated
(shredded) coconut
½ – ¾ tsp cumin seeds
4 tbsp chopped coriander
(cilantro) leaves and stalks
3–4 large mint sprigs, leaves
picked (30–40 leaves)
4–5 green chillies
4–6 garlic cloves, peeled
5 cm (2 in) piece of fresh ginger,
peeled and roughly chopped
1 tsp caster (superfine) sugar
1 tsp salt
juice of ½ lime

To garnish
¼ – ½ tsp cumin seeds

GAJJAR NU ACHAAR

SIMPLE CARROT PICKLE

Makes about 1 kg (2 lb 3 oz)

In the subcontinent a pickle is normally cured in the sun and then stored for eating the following year when the fresh fruit or vegetable comes back into season and a fresh batch is made for the following year. In countries where sunlight is at a premium, we have to use other methods. The tempering/sizzling of spices and, sometimes, cooking the vegetables will ensure that spoilage is minimized and will aid its keeping qualities. This pickle will get better with age and you may prefer to leave one of the jars for a few months to enjoy it at its best.

1 kg (2 lb 3 oz) carrots

1½ –2 tbsp salt

2 tbsp black mustard seeds

1 tsp fenugreek (methi) seeds

1 tbsp cumin seeds

5 cm (2 in) piece of cinnamon stick

5–6 cloves

200 ml (7 fl oz/scant 1 cup) sunflower, rapeseed or olive oil

1 level tbsp ground turmeric

2 tbsp chilli powder

2–3 tbsp caster (superfine) sugar

Peel and cut the carrots into 5 mm (¼ in) batons, 4–5 cm (1½ –2 in) long. Place in a bowl. Sprinkle with the salt, toss well and set them aside for a few hours.

Meanwhile, gently toast the mustard seeds, the fenugreek, cumin, cinnamon and cloves in a dry frying pan for about 30 seconds, stirring, until fragrant. Set aside to cool briefly.

Grind to a powder in a clean coffee grinder or a mortar with a pestle (alternatively use a small bowl with the end of a rolling pin).

Squeeze out all the water from the carrots and place them in a clean (preferably stainless steel) bowl.

Heat the oil in a saucepan until it begins to smoke. Remove from the heat then add all the spices. Keep stirring to prevent them from burning and also to cool the oil rapidly.

Mix the sugar into the carrots and then pour in the oil with the spices. Mix well.

When cold, put in sterilized airtight jars and leave in a cool, dark place for at least a week to allow to mature before eating. The oil will gradually come to the surface and the pickle will soon take on its character.

To ensure the pickle keeps well, when serving always use a dry spoon and, also, as soon as you have taken what you want, wipe the edges with a piece of dry paper towel and then seal again.

HARI CHUTNEY

FRESH GREEN CHUTNEY

Makes 1 small jar

(see image on page 41)

This is one of those chutneys that is made
throughout the subcontinent of India and there
are several versions. In short, green chutney means
using fresh green ingredients with the exception of
some dried spices, which may or may not be added.
Fresh Green Chutney is extremely versatile and
makes an ideal accompaniment for snack items as
well as fresh chargrilled tandoori dishes.

4 tbsp chopped coriander (cilantro)
leaves and stalks

3–4 large mint sprigs, leaves picked
(30–40 leaves)

4–5 green chillies

4–6 garlic cloves, peeled

5 cm (2 in) piece of fresh ginger, peeled
and roughly chopped

1 tsp caster (superfine) sugar

1 tsp salt

juice of ½ lime

Purée all the ingredients together in a food processor until you have a smooth
green paste.

Add a little water, if necessary, for the blades to get a grip on the ingredients but
be careful not to add too much liquid. Stop and scrape down the sides as necessary.

Green chutney can be refrigerated in a sterilized screw-topped jar and will keep
well over two weeks if used carefully with a dry spoon and if the edges of the jar
kept clean.

BHARELA MARCHA NU ACHAAR

WHOLE STUFFED CHILLI PICKLE

Makes about 1 kg (2 lb 3 oz)

Chilli pickles are enjoyed all over the subcontinent. No doubt the chillies differ in size, shape and, above all, in strength. There are numerous types of chilli pickle but this one is easy, quick to prepare and enhances many snacks and curries.

1 tbsp fenugreek (methi) seeds

2 heaped tbsp black mustard seeds

3–4 tbsp sesame seeds

5–6 cloves

5 cm (2 in) piece of cinnamon stick

3 tbsp salt

2 tbsp caster (superfine) sugar

1 tsp ground asafoetida

1 kg (2 lb 3 oz) short, red or green fat chillies

500 ml (17 fl oz/2¼ cups) sunflower or rapeseed oil

Lightly toast the seeds, cloves and cinnamon stick in a small, dry frying pan, stirring for about 30 seconds until fragrant. Pound them to a powder with the salt and the sugar in a clean coffee grinder or a mortar with a pestle (or in a bowl with the end of a rolling pin). Stir in the asafoetida.

Wash and dry the chillies. Slit them down the middle taking care not to cut them open and not letting the knife go through the other side.

Fill each chilli with the spice powder and put them in a stainless steel or a large glass bowl.

Heat the oil in a pan until it begins to smoke. Cool slightly and pour over the chillies whilst still hot.

Keep the chillies in the bowl with a cloth tied over it for 4–5 days before bottling then place in sterilized screw-topped jars, making sure they are totally submerged in the oil.

The chillies need at least a week of maturing but are best left for 10–12 days before beginning to enjoy them. Store in the refrigerator and, if necessary, top up with oil when some are used, then they will keep for up to 6 months.

LASUN CHI TIKHAT

HOT GARLIC CHUTNEY MAHARASHTIAN STYLE

Makes 1 small jar

This is a deliciously simple chutney that goes fantastically well with any meat or poultry dishes. This can be prepared in advance and frozen. Simply defrost a few hours in advance, give it a quick stir and it's ready to go!

10–12 garlic cloves

200 g (7 oz/ 2¼ cups) desiccated (shredded) coconut

1 tbsp cumin seeds

6–8 large dried red chillies

2 heaped tbsp sesame seeds

40 g (1½ oz/¼ cup) raw peanuts

piece of tamarind block, without stones, enough to form a ball the size of a large lime

2 tsp salt

Toast all the ingredients except the tamarind and salt in a dry frying pan, stirring for a minute or two until the coconut and the sesame seeds and peanuts and garlic are browned but not burnt.

Immediately tip into a clean coffee grinder or food processor and grind all the ingredients together. Add the tamarind and salt and process again to a smooth paste, stopping and scraping down the sides as necessary.

Store in a sterilized screw-topped jar in the refrigerator for up to a week.

DESSERTS

Desserts and sweets are a vital part of the Indian diet, be they good or bad for you. Most of what we eat such as *gulab jamuns*, *rusgullas*, *jalaebis*, *rasmalai* etc. are sweets and not necessarily desserts. However, Indian cuisine does produce desserts too, and Bombay is quite the place for some old-time classics, many of these British-influenced, too.

There used to be a place that just made desserts and ice creams when we were young. It was called Jai Hind which simply translated as 'Long Live India', and if you had a bit of change clinking about you could go in and buy jelly and custard, caramel pudding, fruit trifle, baked cabinet pudding, baked bread pudding as well as bread and butter pudding and various ice creams and sundaes. It lost its charm eventually and closed was down by greedy builders who wanted their prime location. Besides Jai Hind, there lies in Bombay a legacy that still exists of some old-time favourites and modern adaptations to please an ever-growing foodie population.

Most Indian desserts are milk-based and often very high in sugar and all the wrong things we are often told to avoid. But the average Indian is still a die-hard sugar freak and will seek out his favourites as we did when we were young, travelling across town in the dead of the night simply to eat at an ice cream parlour that was famous for something like custard apple ice cream.

The legendary Britannia Restaurant in Ballard Pier is to us the best place for great caramel custard (their signature dessert) and rest assured, they can give the best a very, very good run for their money.

Indian desserts have been influenced by the British classics, and dishes like rice pudding, coconut pudding and semolina pudding have all been adapted for Indian palates, spiced and flavoured, giving them their own special twist.

In a typical South Indian restaurant a sweet wheat pudding is served at breakfast known as Cheers which can be part semolina, part whole-wheat flour or all semolina.

If ever in Bombay, be sure to explore the many sweet shops, and our so-called dairies that serve snacks and milk products and banish those health fears for a few moments of over-indulgent and lip-smacking adventues. You could well be lost forever!

Every part of Bombay specialises in something different and you need to know locally where the best *Gajjar ka Halwa* (page 230) is, or the best *aflatoon*, or the best *mawa khaaja* (a delicious flaky pastry sweet which is Bombay's *mille feuille* where reduced sweetened milk is interlayered with puff pastry and baked). You need to be tough to refuse and strong of constitution to digest it all.

1.5 litres (51 fl oz/ 6 cups) whole milk
200 g (7 oz/scant 1 cup) caster
(superfine) sugar
1 tsp natural vanilla extract
4 eggs

CRÈME CARAMEL PUDIM À LA BOMBAY

BOMBAY CARAMEL PUDDING

Serves 6

The British left behind some influences in India's culinary offering and none more so then in the cities of Bombay, Calcutta and Bangalore.

There is still one restaurant in Bombay aptly named Britannia, which makes the best caramel custard ever. Naturally, we could not replicate their recipe exactly, but here is a recipe that represents the taste and flavours we – especially The Parsees – hold dear. Be patient, though, to get that perfect thick, creamy texture and use only the best ingredients.

Heat the milk in a heavy-based, non-stick saucepan and bring to the boil. Reduce the heat and simmer gently until reduced by a third, keeping the sides clean. To do this you need a pastry brush and chilled water. As soon as the milk is simmering, brush the sides with the wet brush. Do this every few minutes to prevent the thickening milk sticking to the pan. Take care not to use a dripping brush, as that is likely to dilute the milk. Also use a flat, preferably wooden, spatula to frequently scrape the bottom to prevent burning. If you notice any formation on the bottom of the pan when you stir, it is advisable to change pans and check rather than to scrape the bottom and end up with burnt bits in the custard.

Don't be impatient and let it happen gradually. Once it is reduced it will be a pale brown and you will notice a great toffee aroma.

Meanwhile, slowly heat 150 g (5 oz/$\frac{2}{3}$ cup) of the sugar in a heavy-based pan with 1 tablespoon of water added until it is a rich golden brown, without stirring (if you stir it the sugar will crystallize).

When you get that beautiful amber colour, pour it into a warm, shallow 1.5 -litre (51-fl-oz/ 6-cup) baking dish and quickly tilt and swirl the dish to spread out the caramel. Take care as caramel burns!

Whisk the milk, preferably with a hand blender to help break any solids and cool it to warm.

Preheat the oven to 120°C/240°F/gas ½. Whisk the eggs with 1 heaped tablespoon of the remaining sugar in a large bowl. Gradually whisk in the warm milk until well blended. Never add egg to the milk as it might split.

Whisk in the vanilla then taste and add a little more sugar if liked but remember that the caramel will also add to the sweetness so don't overdo it!

Strain the custard into the caramel-coated dish. Place in a baking tin with enough boiling water to come 1 cm (½ in) up the sides of the dish.

Bake in the oven for about 1 hour until set. It should be wobbly but not wet.

Remove from the oven, take out of the baking tin and leave to cool.

Chill, if liked, before serving as it is or turned out onto a serving plate. Enjoy!

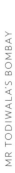

6 blanched almonds, thickly sliced

6–8 blanched and sliced pistachios

8–10 raw cashew nuts, roughly chopped

3 tbsp sunflower oil

1 heaped tbsp sultanas (golden raisins)

2 tbsp butter

100 g (3½ oz/generous ¾ cup) fine to
    medium (not too coarse) semolina

3–4 tbsp caster (superfine) sugar, or to taste

pinch of saffron strands (optional)

750 ml–1 litre (25 fl oz–34 fl oz/
    3–4¼ cups) cold milk

¼ tsp grated nutmeg

¼ tsp ground cardamom

a few drops of natural vanilla extract

1 tsp rose water

a few rose petals (optional)

DOODH NO RAWO

PARSEE SEMOLINA PUDDING

Serves 4–5

Typically Indian too but with the added Parsee extra in flavour and richness!

This is not a woman's recipe but that of a man: mine! It looks dreary but let me assure you that semolina will never taste the same again. Many of us Parsees also add egg yolks to the pudding for added richness, but that's optional. If you only have coarse semolina, whiz it in a food processor or coffee grinder briefly to refine.

Toss the nuts in the oil in a small frying pan over a medium heat. As soon as they are beginning to colour, add the sultanas and toss again. When the nuts are golden brown, remove all with a slotted spoon and place immediately onto paper towels to drain and prevent further cooking.

Add the butter to the drained oil. As soon as it is melted and begins to foam add the semolina. Turn down the heat to medium-low.

With a wooden spoon or flat spatula, stir continuously to toast the semolina for 8–10 minutes until lightly coloured, making sure you loosen it from the corners of the pan where it can stick and burn.

Add the sugar and continue cooking for a further 4 minutes. (You may or may not need more sugar, though I personally do not like it very sweet.)

Remove from the heat to cool slightly for a few seconds. If adding saffron you must first roast the saffron gently in a small pan over a low heat shaking the pan about to distribute the heat evenly. When the saffron strands are crisp, they are ready.

Tip the saffron into the semolina, if using, then add 750 ml (25 ml/3 cups) milk all at once and stir a bit faster now so that no lumps are formed, or whisk it in.

Return to the heat and cook, stirring gently, for 10–12 minutes until the semolina is thick and cooked. If the Rawo is becoming too thick add more milk as desired to make a thick pouring porridge (it will thicken more on cooling so best not to be too thick when hot).

When cooked and the desired consistency, add all the remaining ingredients except the fried nuts, sultanas and rose petals. Cook for a minute or two and check the flavouring. If more milk has been added the flavourings and sugar may need to be increased to suit your taste.

Transfer the mixture to a serving bowl or dish and sprinkle with the fried garnish. Serve warm (but leftover Rawo is great cold the following day).

You can garnish with a few rose petals. Most rose petals are edible and are widely used in India as a garnish on sweets.

GAJJAR KA HALWA

CARROT FUDGE PUDDING

Serves 4

Probably the best known fudge amongst India's
many sweets. It is particularly popular in the North
during winter – just head to the local dairy café
and you will witness lots of people eating fresh, hot
carrot fudge with a cup of freshly brewed tea. It is
tastiest when eaten warm but can be had cold or
eaten at room temperature. Organic carrots are the
best to use and the deeper the colour the better.

Heat the ghee in a heavy-based pan. Add the cardamom seeds and fry for
30 seconds, stirring, until fragrant.

Add the grated carrot and 150 ml (5 fl oz/$2/3$ cup) water and cook, stirring
for 5–10 minutes until tender and almost dry.

Add the milk and keep stirring over a high heat until it starts to boil. Reduce
the heat and simmer gently, stirring frequently, until the milk has almost evaporated
and the mixture is fairly dry. It may take as long as an hour and better not rushed.

Add the sugar and cook, stirring for about 10 minutes until crumbly and fudge-
like. Stir in most of the nuts and raisins. Spoon into serving dishes, sprinkle with
the remaining nuts and raisins and serve hot or cold.

2 (or more) tbsp ghee

6 cardamom pods, split and seeds extracted

500 g (1 lb 2 oz/3⅓ cups) grated carrots

500 ml (17 fl oz/2¼ cups) milk

200 g (7 oz/scant 1 cup) caster (superfine) sugar

2 tbsp chopped, blanched pistachios or almonds

2 tbsp raisins

1.5 litres (51 fl oz/6 cups) whole milk

2 tbsp caster (superfine) sugar,
or to taste

4 eggs

1 tbsp rose water

½ tsp natural vanilla extract

½ tsp ground cardamom

½ tsp grated nutmeg

10–12 blanched almonds, sliced

1 tbsp charoli or toasted pine nuts

10–12 blanched pistachios, sliced

LAGAN NU CUSHTARR

BOMBAY CARAMEL PUDDING

Serves 4–6

A traditional Parsee-style baked custard, a must at festive dinners and at weddings. It's rich and flavourful and its worth using whole milk for the extra-creaminess. If you are watching your weight, go for semi-skimmed instead.

Heat the milk in a heavy-based non-stick saucepan and bring to boiling point. Reduce the heat and simmer gently for about 1 hour until it is reduced by half, keeping the sides clean. To do this you need a pastry brush and chilled water. As soon as the milk is simmering, brush the sides with the wet brush. Do this every few minutes to prevent the thickening milk sticking to the pan. Take care not to use a dripping brush, as that is likely to dilute the milk.

Also use a flat, preferably wooden, spatula to keep scraping the bottom so as not to allow the milk to burn. If you notice any formation on the bottom of the pan when you stir, it is advisable to change pans and check rather than to scrape the bottom and end up with burnt bits in the custard.

Ideally the milk should turn nut-brown and give off a nutty, toffee aroma. When the milk is reduced to about 750 ml (25 fl oz/3 cups), stir the sugar until dissolved. Remove from the heat and allow it to cool for a few minutes.

Beat the eggs in a large bowl. Add a little of the reduced milk and whisk rapidly, then gradually whisk in all the remaining milk (always add the milk to the egg, never the egg to the milk).

Taste and add more sugar if desired, then stir in the rose water, vanilla, cardamom and nutmeg. Whisk well or, better still, use a hand blender to get a really smooth texture.

Preheat the oven to 180°C/350°F/gas 4. Strain the mixture into a 1 litre (34 fl oz/4¼ cup) baking dish.

When you are ready to bake it, sprinkle the nuts evenly over the surface. For best results place the dish in a baking tin containing 1 cm (½ in) boiling water. This will prevent the custard from baking too rapidly and curdling.

Bake for 10 minutes then reduce the heat to 160°C/320°F/gas 3 and cook for 40 minutes or until set or when the tip of a knife inserted in it comes out clean. The colour on top needs to be golden. If not, and the pudding is cooked, gently brush a little melted butter on the surface and place under a moderate grill (broiler) to brown. You may have to rotate the dish to get an even colour.

Leave to cool until warm or completely cold so the custard sets firm before cutting into pieces.

500 ml (17 fl oz/⅔ cups) thick,

   pinch of saffron strands

1 tbsp milk

3–4 tbsp caster (superfine) sugar

1 tsp ground cardamom

1 tsp rose water

8–10 blanched almonds, sliced

8–10 blanched pistachios, sliced

1 tbsp charoli or toasted pine nuts

SHRIKHAND

STRAINED YOGHURT DESSERT

Serves 4–6

Shrikhand is a hugely popular Indian dessert.
It is made across the length and breadth of
the subcontinent. What may be different from
region to region is the flavouring, the addition
of nuts and the sweetness. It can be served
with pooris (see pages 180 or 189) or on its own.
It's very rich, so serve small portions!

Place the yoghurt in a clean disposable kitchen cloth or muslin and tie the open
ends loosely.

Hang the bag now created over the kitchen sink or a bowl for 2–3 hours until all
the liquid has drained. It can also be left in the refrigerator suspended over a bowl
overnight if more convenient.

Meanwhile, toast the saffron strands briefly in a small dry frying pan, tip into a
cup and add the milk. Leave to infuse until the yoghurt is ready.

Tip the drained curds into a large bowl and scrape off any bits sticking to the
cloth. Beat well with a small whisk making sure you scrape the edges with a spatula
and beat again until smooth. Beat in the sugar until it has completely dissolved.

Sprinkle over the ground cardamom and mix it in.

Now add the saffron milk and the rose water and taste. If you need more sugar
then remove a little of the shrikhand and beat the sugar into that until dissolved
then mix with the rest of the dessert.

Transfer the mixture to an attractive serving bowl and sprinkle with the nuts. Chill
well before serving.

DRINKS

'Drinks' is a wide term indeed but here we refer to non-alcoholic drinks and of these there are many, to be found across the length and breadth of the nation.

For those who have visited Bombay they might have often wondered what those little hand-pulled carts are selling. Their beverages are absolute poison for those with weak bellies and even though the term 'Delly Belly' might sound like our capital city Delhi, the Bombay Belly is also very possible! You're better off going to reputed or good decent restaurants and have some drinks there (or making your own, of course).

Limbu Paani (page 242) or fresh lime water is the best thirst-quencher. Besides giving you a shot of vitamin C, it can also come loaded with tons of sugar. Ask for the sugar and salt to be separate and if you mix the two you often get a superb rehydrating drink. Ideally ask for it to be made with soda water as then the water is even more pure. A dash of roasted crushed cumin seeds adds a zest to it and most of us also like it with a smattering of black salt as well.

Sugar cane juice, is a fabulous pure drink crushed straight out of fresh sugar cane and mixed with ginger root to give you a natural energy boost that will knock your socks off.

Indians love their spiced buttermilk in summer, and Lassi (page 249), a richer slightly diluted yoghurt with either sugar or salt, or even a Masala Lassi (page 254). Lassi too is something most people now know about and it is no longer something exotic.

Solkadi (page 245) is commonly sold in coastal Indian restaurants and is a fabulous reinvigorating drink made with extracting the pulp of butternut berries blended with fresh coconut milk and often sizzled with asafetida and mustard seeds. We love it, some hate it, but it's good for you regardless.

However, how can one ever forget the one beverage that unites all of India (except maybe some regions of south India where coffee might take precedence!) *Masala Wali Chai* (page 256), milky chai, *paani cum chai* and of course the fabulous 'first flush' or superior teas sold in five-star hotels but never on the streets. Street chai is made from tea dust (finely ground tea leaves) and is boiled to death to attain that rich dark thick fluid which when blended with milk and boiled is the Bombawalla's Chai. The Portuguese adopted the word 'Cha' in their dictionary and they always say Cha instead of tea which many Western countries do.

Tea was actually an acronym that was burnt onto tea crates exported from India to signify that they had been checked, tested and was now approved for export. It was thanks to the Portuguese that the British started to drink tea, and thanks to one Portuguese princess who became the queen that the afternoon tea ceremony became a ritual for the rich and high society, eventually transferring itself to all classes but in lesser style and pomp. Catherine of Braganza's marriage to Charles II in 1662 led to Britain becoming a nation of tea drinkers and it was the chests of T.E.A. that came for the Royal family that led them to pronounce the word as 'Tea' and soon of course, the Clippers began to sail backwards and forwards bringing with them rich cargoes of tea.

Tea for me is staple and to me a cuppa anytime of the day or night is a welcome sight, but for me its a blend that our family has had since I was a little fellow and used to buy it for my mum and as a result it has stuck for good.

juice of 1–2 limes
(you need about 2 tbsp)
2–3 tbsp caster sugar
pinch of salt
pinch of ground cumin (optional)
1 tbsp water
chilled still, sparkling or soda water

LIMBU PANI

FRESH LIME WITH WATER OR SODA

Serves 1

You can see this being sold in almost every main
street of every major city in India. Fresh limewaters
are very popular like lassi but are lighter and more
refreshing. They replace lost fluids in hot summers
and help to control dehydration and nausea brought
about by extreme heat. In India we use black
rock salt – *kala namak* – as it is rich in therapeutic
minerals. It has a distinctive sulphurous flavour –
try it if you can find it!

Pour the lime juice into a glass.

Add the sugar, salt, cumin, if using, and the tablespoon of water. Stir well until
the sugar and salt have dissolved.

Top up with chilled still, sparkling or soda water. Stir and serve chilled.

700 ml (24 fl oz/scant 3 cups) water

6–8 dried kokum

2–3 large garlic cloves, crushed

500 ml (17 fl oz/2¼ cups)

coconut cream

pinch of salt

2 tbsp chopped coriander (cilantro)

leaves

SOLKADHI

A KONKAN DIGESTIVE DRINK WITH KOKUM

Makes 4 glasses

Think of *Solkadhi* (or *sola chi kodi* or *solkodi* as
it's also called) and you think of curry as it is the
perfect drink to serve with one. It is made with dried
kokum, which is known to be very cooling and has
several medicinal properties. They are available
online or in Asian food stores. The drink looks like
a thin milkshake and the colour has a deep rose tint
to it. This recipe is part Goan part Maharashtrian.
Poured over boiled rice, it's a good cure for an
upset stomach. You can use 2 x 400 ml (14 fl oz)
cans of coconut milk instead of the coconut cream
and water.

Boil 500 ml (17 fl oz/2¼ cups) of the water and pour over the kokum in a bowl.
Leave to cool.

When cool either lift out the kokum then squeeze them over the soaking water
to extract as much flavour as possible or, better still, whiz the whole lot in a blender
until the kokum is totally puréed with the water.

Add the garlic to the blender and blitz again.

Blend the coconut cream with the remaining water until smooth. Strain the
kokum and garlic liquid into this coconut milk.

Season and taste. The taste has to be a bit tart or sour but refreshing. Add the
coriander, mix well and chill for about an hour before serving.

54.

200 ml (4 fl oz/½ cup) chilled thick,
   plain whole milk yoghurt
4 ice cubes
good pinch of salt, or caster (superfine)
   sugar to taste

PLAIN LASSI

YOGHURT SMOOTHIE

Serves 1

A lassi is simply a cooling, whisked yoghurt drink.
For the best lassi select the best yoghurt – this is
essential. A good lassi is not good enough with light
yoghurt or fat-free yoghurt. In India buffalo milk
is normally used which yields approximately 10–12
percent fat. You do not have to go to that extent as
then the lassi becomes heavy but, ideally, use whole
milk yoghurt or a low-fat Greek-style will do if you
are watching your fat content. Lassi can be either
sweet or savoury. For a lighter, thinner lassi, use half
yoghurt and half milk.

Put the yoghurt and the ice cubes in a blender. Add the salt or desired amount
of sugar.

Blitz until blended and frothy.

Pour into a glass and serve.

AAM KI LASSI

MANGO YOGHURT SMOOTHIE

Serves 1

Because we use such rich yoghurt, in summer, when the heat is intense, many Indians enjoy a good lassi (particularly mango or other fruit ones) instead of a meal (or they might just go for a light snack). You can make other fruit lassis the same way, using a large handful of strawberries or raspberries, a peeled peach (with the stone removed), or a peeled, seeded papaya. You may like to sharpen your lassi with a squeeze of fresh lime juice, too.

1 fresh mango, peeled and flesh cut in pieces

120 ml (4 fl oz/½ cup) chilled thick, plain whole milk yoghurt

4 ice cubes

a little chilled milk or water (optional)

caster (superfine) sugar (optional), to taste

Put the prepared fruit in a blender with the yoghurt and ice cubes.

Blitz until smooth and frothy. Sweeten to taste with sugar, if liked.

Pour into a glass and sprinkle with the mint or coriander. Serve straight away.

JEERA LASSI

CUMIN YOGHURT SMOOTHIE

Serves 1

Cumin is called *jeera* in Hindi but it didn't seem
worth giving it its British name as the Indian one
works in both languages! The cumin adds a lovely
warm, earthy spice to a simple, plain lassi. It is also
extremely good for upset stomachs, acidity and
general queasiness.

1 tsp cumin seeds

200 ml (4 fl oz/½ cup) chilled thick, plain
whole milk yoghurt

4 ice cubes

generous pinch of salt

Heat a small, dry frying pan. Add the cumin and toast, stirring, for 30 seconds to
1 minute, until deep brown and fragrant. Tip immediately into a mortar or small
bowl. Grind with a pestle or end of a rolling pin to a powder.

Put the yoghurt, ice cubes and salt in a blender and add about three-quarters
of the cumin.

Blitz until blended and frothy.

Pour into a glass, sprinkle with the remaining cumin and serve nice and cold.

MASALA LASSI

SPICED YOGHURT SMOOTHIE

Serves 1

This lassi is full of flavour and delicious as a drink
to accompany any curry or snack meal. It is also
excellent as a digestif, particularly for over-
indulgence or if suffering from an upset stomach.
For a stronger flavour, add the chopped herbs to
the blender and blitz into the drink rather than
using them as a garnish.

Put the yoghurt and all the flavourings except the mint or coriander in a blender.

Blitz until smooth and frothy.

Pour into a glass and sprinkle with the mint or coriander. Serve straight away.

200 ml (4 fl oz/½ cup) chilled thick,
plain whole milk yoghurt
¼ tsp cumin seeds
2 cm (¾ in) piece fresh ginger,
peeled and chopped
small piece of mild, fresh green chilli,
seeded and chopped
pinch of salt
pinch of caster (superfine) sugar
4 ice cubes
a few mint or coriander (cilantro)
leaves, finely chopped

MASALA WALI CHAI

SPICED TEA

Serves 4

This is a basic, classic chai recipe but you can add more! We Parsees love lemongrass and fresh mint in our tea and even here in London you will always find a stash of lemongrass leaves in our freezer. A small piece of lemongrass or a few bruised mint leaves added right at the end before switching off and covering the pot give a fabulous added zing. For both do not add too much as you will then lose the wonderful sweet, spiced flavour of the tea. Another option is to add a 2.5 cm (1 in) piece of well-crushed fresh ginger. It's particularly good for relief of cold symptoms.

Heat the water, milk and the spices in a non-stick saucepan to boiling point. Reduce the heat and simmer for a couple of minutes, then bring it back to the boil.

As soon as it boils add the tea leaves and reduce to a simmer. Cover the pan and remove from the heat.

Leave to stand for 2 minutes until the leaves settle. If sweetening, stir in sugar to taste, then strain and serve. Or strain and serve the tea, handing sugar separately.

500 ml (17 fl oz/2¼ cups) water

250 ml (8½ fl oz/1 cup) whole milk

2–3 green cardamom pods, crushed

2–3 black peppercorns,
coarsely crushed

2–2.5cm (¾–1 in) cinnamon stick

1 tbsp loose tea leaves

caster (superfine) sugar to taste
(optional, but Indians love sweet,
sugary tea)

INDEX

ABOUT THE AUTHOR

CYRUS TODIWALA OBE, DL

From 'chef of genius'* to 'creator of the classiest curries in the City'** this Bombay-born Parsee chef has been called all manner of good things, but the Chef Patron of Café Spice Namasté, Mr Todiwala's Kitchen and The Park Café in Victoria Park East still has his feet very much on the ground … running!

Cyrus Todiwala cooks, teaches, runs three successful restaurants and does more than his fair bit for charity and the community, but his restless, entrepreneurial soul means he never stands still. He has never said no to a challenge, whether it's leaving a secure Executive Chef role in the Taj Group of hotels in Goa 21 years ago to start all over in the UK, or bravely daring to combine flavours, spices and ingredients in ways no other Indian chef has done before.

Cyrus's 'worst kept secret', Khaadraas Club Dinners, held at Café Spice Namasté every four to five weeks, feature heirloom recipes from his mother and aunts in Bombay and India. They've become coveted rituals, introducing his rich Parsee culinary heritage to a wider audience.

In 2011, with his wife Pervin Todiwala, he opened Mr Todiwala's Kitchen, the signature restaurant at the Hilton London Heathrow T5 and in 2013, the Park Café at Victoria Park East, London. Despite being a hands-on chef, he manages to slot in regular appearances on BBC's *Saturday Kitchen* and other media channels, and has written three books: *International Cuisine: India*, *Café Spice Namasté: New Wave Indian Cuisine* and *Indian Summer*. He appears regularly at top food festivals around the world, including Abergavenny Food Festival in Wales, where his hand-made line of gluten-free pickles and chutneys, Mr Todiwala's Splendidly Spicy Pickles and Chutneys, sell out before the end of the show.

A passionate campaigner for sustainability and buying British, Café Spice Namasté's list of green awards includes the Sustainable Food Award from the Corporation of London and a 'Special Achievement Award' for his commitment to the environment from the Footprint Forum.

Today, Cyrus is the proud recipient of a Craft Guild of Chefs' Special Award and has been made Fellow of the Royal Academy of Culinary Arts and the Master Chefs of Great Britain. In 2013, Café Spice Namasté, which he set up with his wife 18 years ago, won the Best Asian Restaurant Business Award at the Asian Business Awards. And Cyrus is one of only a handful of British Asian chefs with an entry in Who's Who.

Cyrus sits on a number of boards including the London Food Board, under the Mayor's office, and the Hospitality Guild. He is a member of the Asian Restaurant Skills Board, which aims to raise the prestige and profile of the Asian cuisine industry as a career choice – a cause very close to his heart, having opened the pioneering Asian & Oriental School of Catering in 2000, which went on to inspire others chefs to open their own training restaurants. Ever the innovator, ten years later, in 2013, Cyrus launched The Asian Junior Chefs Challenge, a first of its kind, with the Master Chefs of Great Britain, to help introduce Asian cookery to a new generation of homegrown talent. He is an active Ambassador of Springboard UK, the industry careers charity.

Cyrus was awarded an MBE by HM The Queen in 2000 for services to education and training and an OBE in 2009 for his contribution to the hospitality industry. He is also a Deputy Lieutenant of Greater London. In 2012, he cooked the very first luncheon for HM The Queen's Diamond Jubilee Tour, featuring his now famous 'Country Captain' shepherd's pie.

Cyrus is married to Pervin Todiwala, his equal partner in the family business (among other things!), and they have two sons.

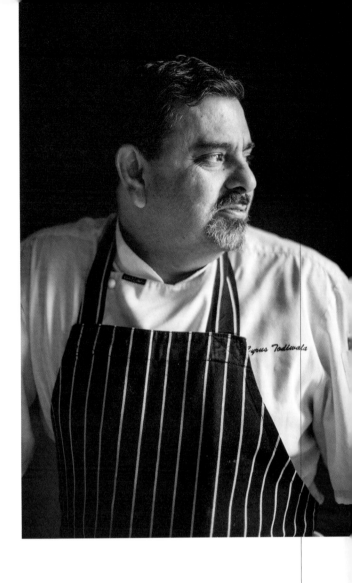

Cyrus's additional honours, awards and citations

Deputy Lieutenant, Greater London

Honorary Doctor of Business Administration,
   London Metropolitan University

Honorary Professor, London School of Tourism,
   Hospitality & Leisure (University of West London)

Springboard Special Award

Cateys Education & Training Award

ITV Tio Pepe Award, 'Outstanding Contribution to London Restaurants'

British Curry Awards Industry Personality of the Year

Culinary Honour of Merit – Epicurean World Master Chefs Society

Best Indian Chef in the UK

BIBA Restaurant Personality of the Year

Arena Accolade

London Evening Standard 1000 Most Influential List – 2010

London Chamber of Commerce & Industry Leadership
   in Sustainability Award – 2011

2011 Corporation of London Sustainable Food Award
   – awarded to Café Spice Namasté

Footprint Awards 2012 – Special Achievement Award

Power 101 List of Most Influential British Asians – 2012

Footprint Awards 2013 – Stakeholder Engagement Award
   – Runner Up – awarded to Café Spice Namasté

Fellow of The Institute of Hospitality

Fellow of the Royal Society of Arts

Fellow of The World Epicurean Master Chefs Society

*By Harpers & Queen

** By Charles Campion

Everyone needs people around them to help them get to their next destination, or chapter in life and I have a lot of people I have depended on that I need to thank. If I were to begin to write it all down I guess a new book would be in the offing!

First of all one needs to thank one's heritage and since Mum and Dad and my extended family are all mentioned I do owe them a deep, deep gratitude and many thanks for allowing me to follow the profession that has given me so much in life. I am also so grateful to them for imparting their knowledge and skills and for being a major part of the support mechanism that has allowed me to learn so much that I can now, myself, share with the world.

Secondly, without the backup support and absolute commitment from my wonderful wife Pervin, I would not have got very far. She maintains the equilibrium and organizes everything for me. This has to include all the hundreds of classes I do across, not just Britain, but as far afield as the USA, Dubai, The Far East, Europe, Brazil and South Africa, and then to be there after me to finish all my work – including this book!

My team in the kitchen has to be given full credit for what I've achieved. Namely, chefs Mathias, Manpreet, Raju and Mehboob who take on the extra burden when I am pre-occupied, or simply have to do all my *Mise-en-place* (organising and preparation of ingredients), and wait for me to finish all the pickles, chutneys, speciality dishes and so on. Without them my creativity and the huge and diverse menus that we produce simply would not be possible (and all those farmers, fishermen and producers across Britain – who often depend on people like us to get their produce rolling – would have no need to contact me!).

But for this book it has to be said that our very dear friend Mahrukh Panthakey, who runs one of Britain's Leading Lasik Eye Clinics with her husband, has given an immense amount of her time to help in formatting the recipes, corrections that I might have overlooked and simply helping me from managing not to delete all my files again, being the computer illiterate chef that I am. She is a Mac expert and that is such a boon.

Next, my thanks to Binay, Ijjath and the Restaurant team for their unfailing support, and to Gina, our wonder literary maestro, who writes so well and keeps us fully linked in with the world around us. I run everything past her and she just glides her watchful eye over the words and spins her magic on them when necessary. A very wise friend, Professor Dr. Ismail Laher, Head of Sciences at the University of British Columbia said, 'Gina can make a stream feel like a great river with her words.'

Last, and by no means least, I'd like to thank the Hardie Grant team – in particular, Stephen King, Kate Pollard and Kajal Mistry – for being patient with me as I scurry around at a million miles an hour trying to please everyone, as well as getting this book ready. Their support, I hope, will pay off and they will reap the benefits of a fabulous book, which they will be proud to have publishe

(I must mention the persistence of Anna Louise and Debbie who kept telling them not to worry as I would do it in time). I am very grateful to Helen, the massively talented photographer who will be giving authors, publishers and chefs like me the privilege of working alongside her for many years to come.

Also, a huge thank you to Charlotte Heal, for her outstanding design skills – there is no denying that this is a spectacularly designed book in which she has managed to bring the majestic charm of Bombay and its food to life.

To my readers and followers, I hope we have brought to you a book that you will treasure and use for many years to come. In five years time, do let me know how many stains accumulate on your copy, (my cousin's wife, Nalini, always shows me my first book, which she has used a million times … and it shows!).

Have fun all
Cyrus

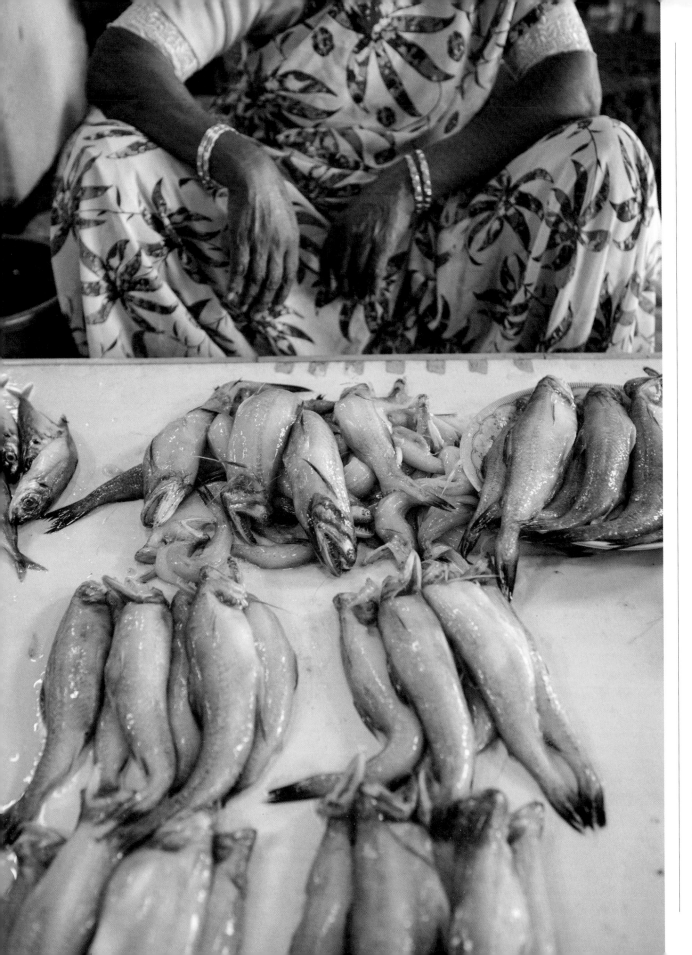

ACKNOWLEDGEMENTS

Mr Todiwala's Bombay 2013 by Cyrus Todiwala

First published in 2013 by Hardie Grant Books

Hardie Grant Books London

Dudley House, North Suite

34–35 Southampton Street

London WC2E 7HF

www.hardiegrant.co.uk

Hardie Grant Books (Australia)

Ground Floor, Building 1

658 Church Street

Melbourne, VIC 3121

www.hardiegrant.com.au

British Library Cataloguing-in-Publication Data. A catalogue record
for this book is available from the British Library.

ISBN 978-1-74270-633-7

Commissioning Editor – Kate Pollard

Desk Editor – Kajal Mistry

Editors – Carolyn Hymphries and Laura Nickoll

Art Direction and Design – Charlotte Heal

Photography and Retouching – Helen Cathcart

Food Styling: Rosie Birkett

Colour Reproduction by p2d

Printed and bound China by 1010 Printing International Limited

10 9 8 7 6 5 4 3 2 1